Chapter 1: Introduction to Faraday Cages and Their Relevance to AI

In today's increasingly connected and digitized world, the need for secure and efficient protection from electromagnetic interference (EMI) has never been more critical. Enter the Faraday Cage: a structure designed to shield its contents from external electric fields and electromagnetic radiation. First discovered by Michael Faraday in 1836, this ingenious concept has evolved from its theoretical origins into a cornerstone of modern electromagnetic protection. Whether in the realm of personal privacy, national security, or cutting-edge technology, Faraday Cages play a vital role in safeguarding the integrity of sensitive systems.

At the same time, artificial intelligence (AI) is reshaping industries, enabling smarter devices, and streamlining complex processes. The synergy between Faraday Cages and AI has the potential to redefine our approach to cybersecurity, privacy, and even space exploration. This book explores the intersection of these two domains—Faraday Cages and AI—demonstrating how they complement each other to create safer, more efficient systems across numerous applications.

Defining the Faraday Cage

A Faraday Cage, at its core, is an enclosure made of conductive material that blocks external static and non-static electric fields. The metal structure essentially forms a shield around whatever is enclosed within, preventing electromagnetic waves from penetrating or disturbing the inner environment. Faraday, the pioneering scientist for whom the cage is named, demonstrated that a conducting surface could protect its contents from external electric fields by redistributing electric charge on the surface, leaving the interior unaffected.

While Faraday's original experiments were quite rudimentary, the principles he discovered have been refined and applied in countless ways. Faraday Cages are now essential components in devices ranging from the shielding of sensitive electronics to the isolation of high-security areas like military installations, data centers, and hospitals.

Faraday Cages in Modern Science and Technology

In the modern era, Faraday Cages have found applications in a variety of fields, including telecommunications, cybersecurity, space exploration, healthcare, and even personal privacy. The proliferation of wireless technology has made shielding against electromagnetic radiation more important than ever. Faraday Cages are integral to preventing the interception or distortion of critical signals and ensuring that systems are not disrupted by unwanted electromagnetic noise.

In telecommunications, Faraday Cages are used to protect sensitive equipment from both natural and artificial sources of interference, such as solar flares and cyberattacks. In the realm of cybersecurity, these cages provide a physical barrier to safeguard against hacking attempts that might exploit electromagnetic waves to breach secure systems.

Space technology also benefits greatly from Faraday Cage principles. Satellites and space stations rely on Faraday Cages to protect their electronic systems from the intense radiation and electromagnetic interference encountered in space. Even astronauts in deep space need Faraday Cage-like protection to shield them from the harmful effects of cosmic radiation.

The versatility of Faraday Cages makes them indispensable in a world increasingly reliant on electromagnetic systems, whether for communication, healthcare, or even military operations.

The Role of AI in Advancing Faraday Cage Applications

The convergence of AI and Faraday Cages presents a powerful opportunity for improving the design, construction, and application of shielding technologies. AI can help identify new materials that enhance the performance of Faraday Cages, optimize their shapes and sizes for specific use cases, and predict how they will behave under various electromagnetic conditions.

For instance, machine learning algorithms can analyze vast datasets to determine the most effective materials for constructing Faraday Cages, ensuring maximum electromagnetic shielding without compromising on weight or cost. AI can also simulate the performance of Faraday Cages in virtual environments, allowing for rapid prototyping and testing without the need for expensive physical models.

Furthermore, AI can be employed to monitor and maintain Faraday Cages, automatically detecting faults or weaknesses in their shielding capabilities. Through real-time analysis and predictive maintenance, AI could significantly enhance the longevity and reliability of Faraday Cage systems.

The Synergy Between Humans and Artificial Intelligence

At its heart, the relationship between humans and AI is one of augmentation—AI is a tool designed to enhance human capabilities, not replace them. When combined with Faraday Cage technology, AI provides a unique opportunity for humans to take their understanding and implementation of electromagnetic shielding to new heights.

Consider the task of optimizing a Faraday Cage for a specific environment, such as a hospital that needs to shield sensitive medical equipment from interference. A human engineer might understand the basic principles of Faraday's law and be able to design a basic protective cage. However, AI can quickly analyze vast amounts of data—ranging from electromagnetic field strength in the area to the optimal material composition—and make precise recommendations that the human engineer might miss. This partnership between human ingenuity and AI-driven analysis can lead to more effective and efficient Faraday Cages.

The integration of AI into the design and implementation of Faraday Cages also promotes safety. Faraday Cages, when properly constructed, offer protection against electromagnetic radiation and other forms of interference that could potentially disrupt or damage crucial systems. However, improperly designed or malfunctioning Faraday Cages can pose risks. AI-driven monitoring systems can ensure that these shields maintain their integrity over time, alerting personnel to any potential vulnerabilities before they result in a breach.

AI can also play a role in making Faraday Cages smarter. For example, as the need for "smart cities" grows, urban infrastructure might rely on AI-managed Faraday Cages to protect both critical communications networks and personal data. The synergy between AI and Faraday Cages thus lays the foundation for a more secure, privacy-conscious, and technologically resilient future.

The Road Ahead: Faraday Cages, AI, and the Future of Protection

The importance of Faraday Cages in modern society cannot be overstated, especially as our world becomes increasingly reliant on wireless communication and connected devices. The ability to shield sensitive information from electromagnetic interference and cyber threats is critical to ensuring both the security of our digital assets and the safety of our physical environments.

Artificial intelligence, with its ability to process data and automate complex processes, is perfectly positioned to enhance the capabilities of Faraday Cages, creating smarter and more efficient shielding systems. The future promises even more advanced uses of AI, from designing next-generation materials to automating the maintenance of Faraday cages in complex environments such as data centers, military installations, and space missions.

As we move further into the 21st century, the synergy between Faraday Cages and AI will become even more integral to the way we protect our digital and physical worlds. By mastering this powerful combination, we can ensure that the technologies we create not only perform as intended but do so safely and securely, safeguarding our privacy, our systems, and our future.

This introductory chapter sets the stage for an in-depth exploration of how Faraday Cages and artificial intelligence intersect, transforming how we approach the challenges of shielding, security, and privacy in an interconnected world.

Chapter 2: The Science Behind Faraday Cages

Faraday Cages are a fundamental tool in modern science and technology, providing protection against electromagnetic fields (EMFs) and ensuring the safety and reliability of electronic systems. Understanding how Faraday Cages work requires a deep dive into the science of electromagnetism, electrostatics, and materials science. In this chapter, we explore the principles behind Faraday Cages, how they operate, the types of materials that can be used, and why AI is a perfect match for advancing their design and functionality.

Electrostatics and Electromagnetic Fields (EMF)

To understand how a Faraday Cage functions, it is essential first to grasp the concepts of electrostatics and electromagnetic fields. Electrostatics refers to the study of stationary electric charges and their interactions, while electromagnetic fields (EMFs) encompass both electric and magnetic fields that oscillate as waves through space. EMFs are present all around us, emanating from various sources such as power lines, electronic devices, communication systems, and even natural sources like the sun.

Electromagnetic interference (EMI) occurs when these fields disrupt the operation of sensitive electronic equipment. This can range from minor malfunctions, like a GPS system losing its signal, to more severe effects, such as damaging data stored on computers or interfering with military communications. Faraday Cages are designed to block or shield sensitive systems from such interference, ensuring the integrity and functionality of the systems inside.

How Faraday Cages Work: The Physics of Protection

At its core, a Faraday Cage works on a relatively simple principle: when a conductive material surrounds a space, it redistributes electromagnetic fields and prevents them from penetrating the interior. This phenomenon occurs because of the behavior of electric fields in conductors.

In the presence of an external electric field, free electrons in a conductor move, redistributing themselves in such a way that the electric field inside the conductor cancels out the external field. This creates a "shielded" region inside the conductor where the electric field is effectively neutralized. The result is that whatever is inside the cage—whether it is a person, a piece of equipment, or sensitive data—remains unaffected by external electromagnetic disturbances.

A key concept in Faraday Cages is that they don't block electromagnetic waves in the traditional sense but rather alter their paths, redirecting them around the shielded area. The effectiveness of a Faraday Cage depends on factors like the material's conductivity, the thickness of the material, and the size of the openings in the cage.

Types of Faraday Cages: Materials and Design Principles

Faraday Cages can take many forms, from simple metal enclosures to complex, multi-layered structures. The choice of materials is critical to the cage's performance. Common materials used for constructing Faraday Cages include:

- **Copper**: Known for its excellent conductivity, copper is one of the most commonly used materials in Faraday Cages. It provides a high degree of electromagnetic shielding and is often used in high-performance applications like sensitive electronics or laboratory environments.

- **Aluminum**: A lightweight, cost-effective material, aluminum is frequently used in commercial Faraday Cages. It is also widely used in shielding mobile phones and other consumer electronics.

- **Steel**: For larger or more robust shielding needs, steel is a popular choice due to its durability and strength. It is often used in industrial applications and military installations.

- **Specialized Alloys**: In some cases, materials such as Mu-metal (an alloy composed primarily of nickel) are used when extra shielding against low-frequency electromagnetic fields is needed.

The design of a Faraday Cage also impacts its effectiveness. A cage with large holes or gaps in its structure will allow electromagnetic waves to enter, reducing its shielding effectiveness. Therefore, ensuring that the cage is as seamless and continuous as possible is crucial for optimal performance. In many applications, the cage may be supplemented with a conductive mesh to further enhance its shielding capacity.

Why AI and Faraday Cages Are a Perfect Match

The integration of artificial intelligence into the design and application of Faraday Cages opens new frontiers in both functionality and precision. AI's ability to process large amounts of data, predict patterns, and optimize designs makes it an invaluable tool in advancing Faraday Cage technology.

AI in Material Selection and Optimization

Selecting the right materials for a Faraday Cage can be a complex task, especially when considering factors like weight, cost, conductivity, and resistance to environmental stressors. AI can assist in material selection by analyzing extensive datasets of material properties and their interaction with different electromagnetic frequencies. Machine learning algorithms can predict which materials will perform best for specific applications, reducing trial and error and improving the speed of innovation.

AI can also optimize the design of Faraday Cages by simulating how various materials and configurations will interact with electromagnetic waves. This allows engineers to test and refine their designs before physically building them, saving both time and resources. For example, AI-driven simulations can model how a Faraday Cage will shield against specific electromagnetic frequencies, allowing designers to make adjustments to the material thickness or mesh size as needed.

Machine Learning for Predicting Interference Patterns

Faraday Cages are typically designed to block specific types of electromagnetic interference (EMI), but they must be tailored to the particular environment in which they are used. AI can be utilized to monitor and map local electromagnetic environments, using machine learning to predict the types of interference a Faraday Cage will encounter.

For instance, machine learning algorithms can analyze data from electromagnetic surveys and use predictive models to forecast how external sources of EMI (such as nearby communication towers, power lines, or industrial machinery) will interact with the cage. These insights allow for more precise engineering of Faraday Cages that are tailored to specific operational environments, such as military bases, hospitals, or data centers.

AI–Based Simulations for Faraday Cage Efficiency

One of the most significant challenges in Faraday Cage design is ensuring that the cage provides sufficient shielding while maintaining other essential properties, such as airflow, weight, and cost. AI-powered simulation tools can rapidly analyze the trade-offs between these factors and generate optimized designs that achieve the desired performance without unnecessary complexity or expense.

For example, AI simulations can evaluate the effects of different material thicknesses, mesh sizes, or structural configurations on the cage's shielding effectiveness. The AI can then recommend the most efficient design, factoring in environmental constraints such as available space or budget limitations. This streamlines the design process and allows for faster development of highly effective Faraday Cages.

Automated AI Systems for Testing and Maintenance

Once a Faraday Cage has been designed and built, AI can play a crucial role in ensuring its ongoing effectiveness. AI-driven testing systems can monitor the cage's shielding performance in real-time, detecting any degradation in the materials or design. By analyzing data from sensors placed within the cage, AI systems can identify areas where the cage may be vulnerable to electromagnetic leakage or failure.

Moreover, AI systems can automate the maintenance process by scheduling inspections, managing repairs, and predicting when certain components (such as shielding materials) may need to be replaced. This proactive approach helps to extend the life of Faraday Cages and ensures they continue to perform optimally, even in demanding environments.

The Future of Faraday Cages and AI Synergy

The fusion of AI with Faraday Cage technology marks the beginning of a new era in electromagnetic protection. AI's ability to simulate, predict, and optimize designs will lead to the creation of more efficient, cost-effective, and adaptable Faraday Cages that can meet the growing demands of our interconnected world.

Whether it's protecting critical infrastructure, ensuring personal privacy, or safeguarding space missions, the integration of AI and Faraday Cages holds immense potential for advancing the technology in ways we've only begun to imagine. In the next chapters, we'll explore specific applications of this powerful combination, demonstrating how AI-driven Faraday Cages are revolutionizing industries from cybersecurity to space exploration and beyond.

This chapter serves as a foundation for understanding the scientific principles behind Faraday Cages, providing context for their role in protecting against electromagnetic interference. With AI's assistance, the potential of Faraday Cages will only continue to grow, unlocking new possibilities for both security and innovation.

Chapter 3: The Evolution of Faraday Cages in History

The Faraday Cage, named after British scientist Michael Faraday, has undergone significant transformation since its discovery in the 19th century. From its humble origins as a basic tool to shield against static electricity to its modern use in protecting against complex electromagnetic interference (EMI), the Faraday Cage has evolved to meet the needs of an increasingly connected world. In this chapter, we explore the historical development of Faraday Cages, their early applications, and the pivotal role AI is playing in revolutionizing Faraday Cage technology today.

The Discovery of the Faraday Effect

Michael Faraday's pioneering work in the early 1800s laid the foundation for much of modern electromagnetic theory. Faraday's key insight came when he discovered that an electric field could be shielded by a conductor. He demonstrated that when a charged conductor—such as a metal enclosure—was placed around an area, the electric field within the enclosure became neutralized. This effect, which he dubbed the "Faraday Effect," was a breakthrough in understanding how electric fields interact with conductive materials.

Faraday's experiments with electric fields and their shielding properties set the stage for the development of the Faraday Cage. The Faraday Cage itself, however, wasn't an immediate invention; rather, it was an extension of his discoveries about electromagnetism. Faraday's work culminated in the creation of a simple metal mesh enclosure that effectively shielded its contents from external electric fields. This marked the birth of the Faraday Cage as we know it today.

Early Applications and Development

In the decades following Faraday's discovery, the applications of Faraday Cages were primarily confined to academic and scientific circles. The early use of Faraday Cages focused on experiments involving static electricity, where the cages were used to protect delicate instruments from external electrical influences. These early cages were typically made of metal sheets or meshes, and they provided a simple yet effective solution to the problem of electrostatic interference.

However, as the world entered the 20th century, the Faraday Cage began to take on new roles, driven largely by advances in the study of electromagnetism and the increasing prevalence of electrical devices. The rise of radio and telecommunication technologies, for instance, highlighted the need to protect sensitive equipment from radio frequency interference (RFI) and electromagnetic interference (EMI). This led to the development of more specialized Faraday Cages designed to shield against these new forms of electromagnetic radiation.

One of the first large-scale applications of Faraday Cages in communication was during the early days of radio broadcasting. Engineers began to realize that electromagnetic waves from one radio transmitter could interfere with the signals of another, causing distortion and loss of communication quality. Faraday Cages were used to shield radio equipment, ensuring clearer signals and reducing cross-talk between stations.

The Rise of Modern Uses in Communications and Security

By the mid-20th century, the role of Faraday Cages expanded beyond the realm of scientific experimentation and radio communication. As the world became more technologically dependent, the need for protection from electromagnetic interference became more critical. In particular, the rise of electronic computing and telecommunications, followed by the explosion of consumer electronics, brought new challenges in the form of unwanted electromagnetic radiation.

Faraday Cages began to be used in a variety of applications, such as:

- **Military and Defense**: The military has long relied on Faraday Cages to protect sensitive communications and equipment from enemy jamming or detection. The U.S. military, for instance, employs Faraday Cages to protect radio signals, radar systems, and classified communications from interception or interference. In sensitive installations like command centers or missile silos, Faraday Cages are used to create secure environments where electromagnetic signals cannot penetrate or leak out.

- **Space Exploration**: Space missions rely heavily on Faraday Cages to shield sensitive spacecraft electronics from solar radiation, cosmic rays, and other forms of electromagnetic interference that could disrupt operations. Early space probes and satellites were often encased in Faraday Cages to protect their onboard systems from the harsh electromagnetic environment of space.

- **Consumer Electronics**: As personal electronics such as mobile phones, laptops, and wearables became ubiquitous, the need for shielding against electromagnetic radiation became apparent. Faraday Cages began to be integrated into these devices, either as physical enclosures or as protective layers within the devices themselves, to block unwanted signals and enhance privacy.

The evolution of Faraday Cages during the 20th century was closely tied to technological advancements, which in turn drove innovation in materials and design. The advent of new metals, alloys, and composite materials, coupled with improved manufacturing techniques, allowed for more effective and versatile Faraday Cages. The development of advanced mesh designs, for instance, enabled the creation of lightweight yet highly effective shielding solutions that could be incorporated into a wide range of applications.

AI's Role in Revolutionizing Faraday Cage Technology

While the foundational principles of Faraday Cages have remained largely unchanged, the role of artificial intelligence in enhancing their design, material selection, and functionality marks the dawn of a new era. AI is catalyzing the next wave of Faraday Cage innovations, bringing new capabilities and applications to the forefront.

AI-Driven Design Optimization

Modern Faraday Cages are no longer limited to simple metallic boxes; they are increasingly sophisticated and tailored to specific needs. AI plays a key role in optimizing Faraday Cage design. Machine learning algorithms can now analyze vast amounts of data to predict the most effective materials, dimensions, and configurations for a given application. These AI-driven models can simulate the behavior of electromagnetic fields within different Faraday Cage designs, allowing engineers to fine-tune their designs to achieve maximum shielding effectiveness while minimizing material costs and weight.

For example, AI can model how different mesh sizes, materials, and geometries will interact with various electromagnetic frequencies. By processing this data, AI tools can suggest optimal design configurations that balance performance with practical constraints, such as space limitations, cost, and environmental factors.

AI in Materials Research and Development

The performance of a Faraday Cage is heavily dependent on the materials used in its construction. AI is revolutionizing material science by accelerating the discovery of new materials with superior electromagnetic shielding properties. AI models can predict the properties of materials based on their molecular composition and structure, allowing researchers to identify novel materials that could provide better performance than traditional metals.

In addition, AI can help optimize the use of existing materials by analyzing how they interact with electromagnetic fields. For example, AI algorithms can evaluate the conductivity, permeability, and thickness of materials to determine how best to combine them in a multi-layered Faraday Cage design. This process not only improves shielding performance but also reduces the environmental impact of Faraday Cage construction by minimizing the use of rare or harmful materials.

Real-Time Monitoring and Maintenance

AI is also improving the maintenance and operation of Faraday Cages. Traditional Faraday Cages are static in nature; once they are built, they often remain unchanged until they are dismantled or replaced. However, with the integration of AI-driven sensors and monitoring systems, Faraday Cages can now provide real-time feedback on their performance.

AI can continuously monitor the electromagnetic environment inside and outside the Faraday Cage, detecting any fluctuations in shielding effectiveness. If the system detects degradation, such as wear and tear on the materials or changes in the electromagnetic environment, it can automatically alert operators and suggest corrective actions. This type of predictive maintenance reduces downtime and ensures that Faraday Cages continue to operate at peak efficiency.

The Future of Faraday Cages and AI Synergy

Looking ahead, the relationship between Faraday Cages and AI is set to evolve in even more transformative ways. AI is likely to play an increasingly important role in developing the next generation of Faraday Cages, including fully autonomous systems that can adapt to changing electromagnetic environments in real time. These AI-enhanced Faraday Cages could be capable of adjusting their shielding properties dynamically based on detected electromagnetic activity, offering unparalleled protection.

Moreover, as the Internet of Things (IoT), autonomous vehicles, and other connected technologies become more prevalent, the need for advanced Faraday Cages to shield sensitive equipment will only grow. AI will be at the heart of this evolution, driving innovations that will keep pace with the ever-expanding digital landscape.

The evolution of Faraday Cages, from their initial conception in the 19th century to their modern applications in communications, security, and space exploration, has been marked by the continual quest to protect against the growing threats posed by electromagnetic interference. As we look to the future, the integration of AI will undoubtedly propel Faraday Cage technology to new heights, ensuring that these protective shields remain relevant and effective in an increasingly interconnected world. In the next chapter, we will explore the ways in which AI is helping to revolutionize the design and implementation of Faraday Cages in the digital world.

Chapter 4: Understanding Electromagnetic Fields and Radiation

Electromagnetic fields (EMF) are an inherent aspect of the modern technological landscape, influencing everything from communication systems to healthcare devices. These invisible forces permeate the environment, often in ways that are either beneficial or harmful to devices and humans. As our dependence on electronics and digital infrastructure increases, the need for effective shielding against harmful EMF and radiation becomes ever more critical. In this chapter, we will delve into the basics of electromagnetic fields, explore their impact on devices and human health, and discuss how Faraday Cages, with the aid of AI, provide a powerful solution to these challenges.

Basics of Electromagnetic Fields (EMF)

Electromagnetic fields are generated by the movement of electrically charged particles. These fields consist of two components: electric fields and magnetic fields, which oscillate perpendicular to each other as they propagate through space. EMF can be found in various forms, from the static fields produced by everyday electrical appliances to the dynamic, high-frequency waves emitted by radio transmitters, microwave ovens, and cell phones. The spectrum of EMF spans a vast range, from extremely low-frequency (ELF) waves, such as those emitted by power lines, to higher-frequency radiation like microwaves, infrared, visible light, ultraviolet, and X-rays.

The primary distinction between these different types of EMF is their frequency, which determines their energy levels and how they interact with matter. For instance, low-frequency waves (like those from power lines) are generally less energetic and pose fewer risks to human health, while higher-frequency waves (such as X-rays or gamma rays) carry much more energy and can cause significant biological damage if exposure is prolonged or intense.

How EMF Affects Devices and Human Health

EMF impacts both electronic devices and biological systems, though in different ways. For devices, EMF can lead to electromagnetic interference (EMI), which disrupts the normal operation of sensitive equipment. This interference can cause malfunctions in computers, communication systems, medical devices, and even everyday consumer electronics. As electronic systems become more complex and interconnected, managing and mitigating EMI becomes a growing concern.

For humans, the effects of EMF exposure are a subject of ongoing research and debate. While some forms of low-frequency radiation are considered harmless, prolonged or intense exposure to higher-frequency EMF—such as that from mobile phones or wireless networks—has raised concerns about potential health risks. Some studies suggest that long-term exposure to electromagnetic fields could contribute to issues like cancer, neurological disorders, and reproductive health problems. However, the scientific consensus remains inconclusive, with many regulatory bodies asserting that current exposure limits are safe for the general population.

Despite the uncertainty surrounding health risks, it is clear that EMF, especially from high-frequency sources, can have significant effects on devices, both in terms of functionality and security. The increasing density of EMF sources, as well as the growing use of wireless communication technologies, underscores the need for effective shielding solutions like Faraday Cages.

The Growing Threat of Electromagnetic Interference (EMI)

The proliferation of wireless technologies, including Wi-Fi, Bluetooth, 5G, and satellite communication systems, has dramatically increased the amount of EMF in the environment. While these technologies offer tremendous benefits, they also contribute to an increasingly cluttered electromagnetic spectrum. As more devices emit and receive EMF, the likelihood of EMI—the disturbance caused by unwanted electromagnetic signals—grows, threatening the integrity of communication networks, sensor systems, and even medical devices.

EMI is particularly problematic in environments where precision and reliability are paramount, such as in hospitals, data centers, and military installations. For example, in a hospital setting, electromagnetic interference can disrupt the functioning of life-saving equipment like pacemakers, ventilators, and diagnostic tools, leading to potentially fatal consequences. Similarly, in communication networks, EMI can distort data transmissions, leading to slower speeds, dropped calls, and compromised security.

To protect against these risks, Faraday Cages provide a robust solution by acting as shields that block external electromagnetic signals. The next section will explore how these cages work in detail and why they are so effective at mitigating EMI.

Using AI to Map, Measure, and Control EMF

The role of AI in managing EMF interference cannot be overstated. While Faraday Cages have long been the standard for shielding against EMF, AI is revolutionizing how these barriers are designed, tested, and maintained. By integrating machine learning algorithms, AI can analyze electromagnetic environments in real-time, mapping out areas of high EMI and identifying where shielding is most needed.

AI-Driven EMF Mapping and Analysis

AI-powered systems can process vast amounts of data from EMF sensors to create detailed maps of electromagnetic fields within a given environment. These maps allow for precise identification of high-risk areas where interference is likely to cause problems. By leveraging machine learning models, AI can predict the sources of EMF, track their movement, and estimate the impact on both devices and humans.

For example, in a hospital or data center, AI can identify the precise locations where interference might disrupt critical operations and then suggest targeted solutions, such as enhanced Faraday Cage shielding or repositioning sensitive equipment to minimize exposure. This level of specificity enables organizations to protect their assets more effectively than traditional methods.

AI in Shielding Optimization

AI can also optimize the design and placement of Faraday Cages to enhance their shielding effectiveness. Traditional Faraday Cages are often built with a one-size-fits-all approach, but AI allows for more dynamic and tailored solutions. By running simulations and analyzing data from existing shielding structures, AI can predict how different materials, mesh sizes, and geometries will interact with electromagnetic fields. This leads to the development of Faraday Cages that are both more efficient and cost-effective.

Machine learning models can also be employed to assess the behavior of EMF in real-time, adjusting the properties of a Faraday Cage on the fly. For example, an AI system could automatically adjust the thickness or material composition of a shield depending on the intensity of the electromagnetic fields detected in the environment, providing dynamic protection.

AI-Driven Performance Monitoring and Maintenance

Another advantage of AI integration is the ability to monitor Faraday Cages continuously for any degradation in performance. Faraday Cages, particularly those in high-traffic or high-risk environments, can experience wear over time, diminishing their ability to block electromagnetic fields. AI systems can track performance metrics and trigger maintenance alerts when shielding effectiveness starts to decline.

In addition, AI can assist in the development of self-healing Faraday Cages, where embedded sensors and algorithms detect damage to shielding materials and automatically initiate repairs or adjustments to maintain protection levels. This kind of proactive maintenance is a game-changer for industries that require continuous operation without interruption.

Faraday Cages in the Digital World: A New Era of Protection

As digital infrastructures continue to expand and become more complex, the role of Faraday Cages in protecting both devices and data will grow in importance. In the next chapter, we will delve into how Faraday Cages are being used to safeguard against cybersecurity threats, shield AI systems from interference, and ensure the integrity of IoT devices and communication networks. With the assistance of AI, Faraday Cages are no longer static structures but dynamic systems capable of adapting to the ever-changing digital landscape, offering unparalleled protection in an increasingly interconnected world.

In conclusion, the evolving challenges posed by electromagnetic fields and radiation require innovative solutions. The synergy between Faraday Cages and AI offers a powerful means to protect devices and humans alike from the growing threats of EMF and EMI. As technology continues to advance, the role of AI in designing, optimizing, and maintaining Faraday Cages will only become more critical, ensuring that we can continue to operate securely in an ever-more connected world.

Chapter 5: Applications of Faraday Cages in the Digital World

In the digital age, where data transmission and electronic devices are central to nearly every aspect of modern life, the need for robust protection against electromagnetic interference (EMI) has never been greater. As the world becomes more connected, cybersecurity threats evolve, and our reliance on AI-driven technologies grows, the role of Faraday Cages in the digital world has taken on newfound importance. This chapter explores how Faraday Cages are applied to protect data, shield AI systems from external interference, secure IoT devices and communication networks, and revolutionize the digital ecosystem with AI-driven innovations.

Protecting Data from Cybersecurity Threats

As organizations continue to digitize their operations, the protection of sensitive data has become one of the top priorities. Cybersecurity threats, such as hacking, data breaches, and ransomware attacks, are a constant concern. These threats not only compromise private information but can also disrupt critical operations in industries ranging from healthcare to finance.

Faraday Cages provide a powerful method of shielding sensitive electronic systems from external electromagnetic threats, including attacks designed to exploit vulnerabilities in wireless communication. They act as an impenetrable barrier, preventing unauthorized signals or interference from penetrating the shielded area. For example, in data centers, where vast amounts of sensitive information are stored and transmitted, the use of Faraday Cages ensures that hacking attempts through electromagnetic signals—such as those made through RF (radio frequency) or electromagnetic pulse (EMP)—are thwarted.

Beyond physical protection, AI has emerged as a valuable tool in enhancing the functionality of Faraday Cages. AI-driven systems can continuously monitor electromagnetic interference in real-time and automatically adjust the performance of Faraday Cages to prevent breaches or disruptions. By continuously scanning for vulnerabilities and adapting to new types of attack vectors, AI ensures that data remains secure against both external and internal threats.

Shielding AI Systems from External Interference

AI systems are highly susceptible to electromagnetic interference (EMI), which can significantly affect their performance. Whether deployed in industrial automation, autonomous vehicles, or cloud-based infrastructures, AI-driven systems rely on precise, uninterrupted operation. External electromagnetic interference can distort data inputs or disrupt the computational processes of AI models, leading to errors, inefficiencies, or even catastrophic system failures.

Faraday Cages are an ideal solution for shielding these AI systems from external EMI, ensuring that the integrity of AI algorithms is maintained. For instance, in autonomous vehicles, where AI is responsible for interpreting sensor data, navigation, and decision-making, interference from nearby electrical equipment could compromise the vehicle's ability to respond to changes in its environment. A Faraday Cage can be incorporated into the vehicle's design to protect its internal AI systems from this type of disruption, ensuring that the vehicle functions safely and efficiently.

Similarly, AI-powered infrastructure like smart grids and data processing centers can benefit from Faraday Cages to safeguard against external electromagnetic disruptions. By creating a protective shield around the systems responsible for AI computations and communications, Faraday Cages help to maintain the accuracy and reliability of AI-driven operations in critical sectors.

Securing IoT Devices and Communication Networks

The rise of the Internet of Things (IoT) has dramatically increased the number of connected devices in everyday life, from smart home appliances to industrial sensors. While these devices offer convenience and efficiency, they also present new vulnerabilities, especially in terms of security. The wireless communication protocols used by IoT devices, such as Wi-Fi, Bluetooth, and Zigbee, are susceptible to hacking and interference, which can compromise the privacy of users and the integrity of critical systems.

Faraday Cages offer a reliable solution for shielding IoT devices from external interference, preventing cyberattacks that exploit weaknesses in wireless communication. In industrial settings, where IoT devices control vital systems such as machinery, sensors, and HVAC systems, Faraday Cages can ensure that electromagnetic interference does not disrupt the performance of these devices. This protection is especially important in environments where IoT devices are integrated into critical infrastructures, such as smart cities, healthcare facilities, and energy systems.

For instance, in a smart city, where countless IoT devices are responsible for monitoring traffic, energy usage, and public safety, electromagnetic interference could lead to incorrect data transmission or loss of connectivity. By using Faraday Cages to shield these devices, cities can safeguard their networks against threats that would otherwise jeopardize the smooth operation of essential services.

AI can further enhance the protection of IoT systems by using machine learning algorithms to predict potential points of failure and optimize the placement and configuration of Faraday Cages. AI can also monitor the electromagnetic environment in real time, dynamically adjusting the shielding properties of the Faraday Cage as needed to ensure optimal protection.

AI-Driven Innovations in Faraday Cage Design

The integration of AI into the design and application of Faraday Cages is revolutionizing their effectiveness in protecting digital systems. Traditional Faraday Cages, while effective, can be rigid in their design and construction, relying on pre-defined material choices and configurations. AI, on the other hand, allows for highly customized and adaptive solutions that optimize the shielding properties of Faraday Cages for specific use cases.

AI in Material Selection and Optimization

The performance of a Faraday Cage depends largely on the materials used to construct it. Traditionally, metals like copper, aluminum, or steel have been used due to their high conductivity, which allows them to block electromagnetic fields. However, AI-powered simulations are enabling the exploration of new materials and hybrid solutions that offer superior performance while also reducing cost and weight.

Machine learning algorithms can predict how different materials will interact with electromagnetic waves, allowing for the creation of optimized Faraday Cages that balance performance, durability, and cost-efficiency. For example, AI can analyze and select materials with the right combination of conductivity, permeability, and shielding effectiveness based on the specific frequencies that need to be blocked. This ability to tailor materials to the electromagnetic environment is a game-changer in applications such as military communications, IoT devices, and even consumer electronics.

AI-Based Simulations for Faraday Cage Efficiency

Before constructing a Faraday Cage, AI-based simulations allow engineers to model how electromagnetic fields will interact with the cage's structure. These simulations take into account variables such as frequency range, intensity, and angle of attack, helping to predict the cage's shielding effectiveness. This enables a more efficient and precise design process, reducing the need for physical prototypes and allowing for rapid iteration in response to changing requirements.

For instance, in the design of a Faraday Cage to protect AI-powered devices in a hospital setting, simulations could reveal the optimal size and shape of the cage, as well as the best material choices, to block interference from nearby medical equipment. This AI-assisted approach ensures that Faraday Cages are not only functional but also cost-effective and tailored to their specific applications.

The Future of Faraday Cages in the Digital Ecosystem

The increasing sophistication of digital infrastructure and the proliferation of connected devices will continue to amplify the demand for effective shielding solutions. Faraday Cages, enhanced by AI, are poised to play a critical role in ensuring the security and reliability of digital systems. As AI-driven innovations in material science, simulation, and real-time monitoring continue to evolve, Faraday Cages will become more adaptive, intelligent, and seamlessly integrated into the digital ecosystem.

In the next chapter, we will explore how AI can be utilized to streamline the process of building and testing Faraday Cages, enabling their deployment in diverse environments from data centers to autonomous vehicles. The integration of AI into Faraday Cage technology will not only protect against electromagnetic threats but also shape the future of secure, resilient, and smart systems.

In conclusion, Faraday Cages offer a critical layer of protection against electromagnetic interference in the digital world. By securing data, shielding AI systems, and safeguarding IoT devices and communication networks, they help maintain the integrity and reliability of electronic systems. With AI's support, Faraday Cages are becoming more efficient, customizable, and integrated into our digital infrastructure, paving the way for more secure, resilient, and connected technologies.

Chapter 6: The Role of AI in Faraday Cage Design

The design of Faraday Cages has long been a field rooted in material science, physics, and engineering. Traditional methods for constructing these protective shields relied heavily on trial and error, physical prototypes, and expert intuition. However, with the rapid advancement of artificial intelligence (AI), the design and optimization of Faraday Cages have entered a new era of precision, efficiency, and adaptability. This chapter explores how AI is transforming the field of Faraday Cage design, from material selection and optimization to real-time testing and performance monitoring, and highlights the evolving synergy between humans and AI in this process.

AI in Material Selection and Optimization

The key to an effective Faraday Cage lies in the materials used to construct it. Historically, metals such as copper, aluminum, and steel have been favored for their high electrical conductivity and ability to block electromagnetic radiation. However, the material selection process has traditionally been a trial-and-error process, dependent on experimentation and expert knowledge. With the integration of AI, this process has become more data-driven and optimized.

AI-driven simulations and machine learning algorithms allow engineers to predict the electromagnetic shielding performance of different materials before any physical testing takes place. These algorithms analyze a wide range of material properties—such as electrical conductivity, permeability, and tensile strength—and forecast how they will interact with electromagnetic waves at various frequencies.

For instance, AI tools can quickly evaluate a material's ability to block a specific frequency of electromagnetic radiation, a crucial consideration for applications like protecting sensitive military communications or securing data centers. With AI, materials that may not have been considered in traditional design processes can be explored, opening new possibilities for more effective and lightweight Faraday Cages.

In addition to selecting the right materials, AI can optimize the design of multi-layered Faraday Cages, which use different materials in combination to block a broader range of electromagnetic frequencies. AI can determine the optimal number of layers, the best arrangement of materials, and even recommend hybrid materials that maximize shielding efficiency while minimizing weight and cost.

Machine Learning for Predicting Interference Patterns

One of the biggest challenges in designing Faraday Cages is accounting for the complex nature of electromagnetic fields and interference patterns. Electromagnetic waves vary in terms of frequency, amplitude, and direction, making it difficult to predict how they will interact with different objects and environments. Historically, this has required extensive testing and iterative design processes to achieve optimal shielding.

With the introduction of machine learning (ML) algorithms, Faraday Cage design has become more precise and predictive. ML models can analyze vast datasets of electromagnetic field behavior and interference patterns, learning to predict how different configurations of Faraday Cages will respond to varying environmental conditions. These algorithms can be trained on data from real-world tests, simulations, and historical performance metrics, allowing them to identify the most efficient shielding designs for specific use cases.

For example, an AI model might be trained to understand the specific interference patterns produced by certain types of communication equipment, such as 5G towers or satellite signals. The model can then recommend Faraday Cage designs that are most effective in shielding against these specific types of interference. In scenarios where environmental conditions are constantly changing, such as in military settings or dynamic urban environments, AI's predictive capabilities enable Faraday Cages to be designed with an adaptive, real-time shielding response.

AI–Based Simulations for Faraday Cage Efficiency

Simulating the electromagnetic shielding effectiveness of a Faraday Cage has traditionally been a complex, time-consuming process. Engineers would create a digital model of the cage and then perform computational simulations, a method that required significant computational power and was often limited by the accuracy of the underlying physics models.

AI, particularly deep learning and reinforcement learning techniques, has greatly improved the accuracy and efficiency of these simulations. By training neural networks on vast datasets of electromagnetic behavior and cage configurations, AI can predict the shielding effectiveness of various designs with a much higher degree of accuracy than traditional methods.

These AI-powered simulations also enable engineers to experiment with more creative or unconventional designs that would have been prohibitively time-consuming or expensive to test manually. For instance, AI could suggest unconventional geometries or material combinations that would provide superior shielding while reducing the size and cost of the Faraday Cage.

Moreover, AI can simulate real-world environmental conditions, such as varying levels of interference, temperature fluctuations, or the presence of physical obstacles, allowing for the design of more robust and reliable Faraday Cages that perform well in diverse settings.

Advanced AI Tools in Prototype Testing

While AI-based simulations are invaluable for the design process, physical prototypes are still necessary to ensure that the theoretical designs hold up in real-world conditions. Traditional testing methods, however, can be cumbersome, requiring extensive time and resources to validate each design iteration.

AI accelerates this process through the use of advanced testing tools and automated systems that continuously monitor and analyze the performance of prototypes. For example, AI-driven sensors can be placed within the prototype Faraday Cage to measure its shielding effectiveness across a wide range of frequencies. These sensors can provide real-time feedback on the cage's performance, identifying areas where shielding could be improved.

Machine learning algorithms can also be employed to analyze the data generated during testing and suggest modifications to the design. This iterative process, powered by AI, allows engineers to rapidly refine and optimize their prototypes, reducing the time and cost associated with traditional testing methods.

Additionally, AI can be integrated with robotic systems to perform physical tests automatically, such as exposing the Faraday Cage to different types of electromagnetic radiation and analyzing its response. This automation speeds up the validation process and ensures a more consistent and reliable testing environment.

Incorporating AI Monitoring and Control Features

Once a Faraday Cage is built and deployed, AI continues to play an important role in maintaining and optimizing its performance. AI-powered monitoring systems can continuously track the electromagnetic environment and the performance of the Faraday Cage in real time. These systems can detect any degradation in shielding effectiveness due to wear and tear, environmental changes, or interference from new sources.

For instance, in a high-security data center, AI monitoring systems can detect if a Faraday Cage has been breached or if external electromagnetic interference is compromising the integrity of the data being stored. In such cases, AI can automatically adjust the shielding parameters or alert human operators to take corrective action.

In more dynamic environments, such as transportation networks or autonomous vehicles, AI can use real-time data to adapt the Faraday Cage's shielding properties as conditions change. For example, an autonomous vehicle's Faraday Cage might be adjusted in response to changing electromagnetic interference in its environment, ensuring that its communication systems remain undisturbed and the vehicle continues to operate safely.

The Human–AI Collaboration: A New Frontier in Faraday Cage Design

As AI becomes increasingly integrated into the design and optimization of Faraday Cages, the role of human engineers evolves. Rather than being the sole creators of designs, humans now collaborate with AI systems, guiding their direction and making high-level decisions while AI handles the more granular aspects of material selection, pattern recognition, and testing.

This collaboration between humans and AI allows for a more efficient, innovative, and scalable approach to Faraday Cage design. AI brings speed, precision, and data-driven insights, while human engineers provide the creativity, intuition, and oversight that ensure the final product meets the practical and ethical needs of the application.

As we move into a future where AI and Faraday Cages are increasingly intertwined, this collaboration will be essential for tackling the growing challenges posed by electromagnetic interference, data security, and privacy protection. The fusion of human ingenuity and AI-powered design represents the next frontier in creating more resilient, adaptive, and effective Faraday Cages.

In the next chapter, we will explore how AI-driven Faraday Cages are applied in critical infrastructure, from healthcare facilities to data centers, and examine the role of AI in large-scale shielding solutions. The increasing complexity of global communication systems demands innovative approaches to protection, and Faraday Cages, enhanced by AI, offer an unprecedented level of security and reliability.

Chapter 7: Faraday Cages and National Security

In today's world, national security is no longer confined to military bases, borders, or espionage in the traditional sense. As digital landscapes evolve, the security of sensitive data, communication systems, and national infrastructure is more dependent on technological innovation than ever before. Among these innovations, Faraday Cages—combined with the power of Artificial Intelligence (AI)—emerge as crucial elements in safeguarding critical national assets against electromagnetic threats, cyberattacks, and unauthorized surveillance. This chapter delves into the pivotal role of Faraday Cages in national security, exploring how AI is shaping the future of shielding technologies to protect sensitive communications, encrypted data, and critical infrastructure.

Protecting Sensitive Military Communications

Military communications are foundational to the effective operation of defense forces worldwide. The secure transmission of intelligence, strategic commands, and battlefield information can make the difference between victory and defeat. As the world moves further into the digital age, the electromagnetic spectrum—through which all wireless communications are transmitted—becomes an increasingly vulnerable point of attack.

Faraday Cages provide an essential layer of protection against these electromagnetic vulnerabilities. By enveloping communication systems in a conductive material that blocks external electromagnetic fields, Faraday Cages prevent eavesdropping, hacking, and jamming. For military communications, the need for such shielding is paramount, as interference or interception of messages could jeopardize national security and even lives.

AI-driven advancements are pushing the boundaries of how military Faraday Cages are designed and deployed. AI tools are used to assess electromagnetic vulnerabilities, predict potential interference sources, and optimize the configuration of shielding materials to ensure maximum effectiveness. AI is also helping military leaders monitor the real-time effectiveness of these shielding systems, alerting personnel to any weaknesses or threats that might compromise communication channels.

AI's predictive capabilities also extend to understanding the behavior of electromagnetic radiation in various environments, allowing for adaptive Faraday Cages that automatically adjust their shielding properties depending on the type and source of the threat. This means that Faraday Cages protecting military communication devices can dynamically respond to changes in the electromagnetic landscape, ensuring continuous and secure communications no matter the external interference.

Faraday Cages in Encrypted Communications

Encryption plays a vital role in safeguarding the privacy and integrity of sensitive communications. It is the backbone of secure financial transactions, diplomatic communications, and military operations. However, even the most robust encryption algorithms can be rendered ineffective if the physical security of the devices transmitting encrypted data is compromised.

Faraday Cages are an integral part of the encryption security protocol, particularly for high-stakes applications such as government communications, financial institutions, and intelligence agencies. Enclosing encrypted communication devices in a Faraday Cage ensures that electromagnetic emanations—leaked signals that might be captured and analyzed by unauthorized parties—are blocked. This prevents "side-channel attacks," where an adversary could gain access to encryption keys or other sensitive information without directly hacking the system.

AI plays a crucial role in securing encrypted communication systems protected by Faraday Cages. AI-powered systems can detect even the faintest electromagnetic leaks, enabling swift responses to mitigate potential threats. Furthermore, AI tools can analyze historical data to identify patterns in electromagnetic radiation, improving the design of Faraday Cages for future encrypted communication devices.

In addition to shielding physical devices, AI-enhanced Faraday Cages can also monitor the surrounding electromagnetic environment for signs of potential surveillance, alerting users to the presence of malicious actors attempting to capture or disrupt encrypted communications.

AI in Monitoring and Counteracting Electromagnetic Threats

Electromagnetic threats, such as Electromagnetic Interference (EMI) and Electromagnetic Pulse (EMP) attacks, are a growing concern for national security. EMI can disrupt the functioning of critical electronic systems, while an EMP could potentially disable entire grids of electrical infrastructure, communications systems, and military hardware. The damage caused by such attacks is not only expensive but could be catastrophic for national defense and emergency response systems.

Faraday Cages, especially those designed with AI integration, provide a critical defense mechanism against these threats. AI tools enhance the ability of Faraday Cages to detect, analyze, and mitigate electromagnetic disturbances. By monitoring the electromagnetic spectrum in real time, AI systems can identify emerging threats, predict their potential impact, and adjust shielding parameters accordingly.

AI-driven predictive algorithms also allow for a more proactive approach to electromagnetic threats. By analyzing historical data, machine learning models can identify patterns of EMI or EMP attacks, providing early warnings for potential national security breaches. These models can also simulate the impact of various threat scenarios, helping decision-makers devise better-prepared responses.

Moreover, AI plays an essential role in ensuring the continuous performance of Faraday Cages over time. Real-time AI monitoring systems can detect any weaknesses or degradation in the shielding material, enabling timely maintenance and reinforcing the integrity of electromagnetic protection systems.

The Intersection of Security, AI, and Faraday Shielding

As the digital world becomes increasingly interconnected, the intersection of AI, cybersecurity, and Faraday Cages will become even more significant in national defense strategies. The convergence of these technologies offers an unprecedented level of protection for national security interests. From military communications to secure infrastructure, the synergy of Faraday Cages and AI holds the key to an advanced, adaptive, and resilient defense system.

For example, in a scenario where a national power grid is compromised, AI-integrated Faraday Cages could safeguard critical communication and operational systems from EMP-induced failure. AI algorithms would quickly identify the EMP signature, instantly activating Faraday Cages in high-priority sectors to prevent radiation from reaching sensitive infrastructure. This level of coordination between AI systems and Faraday shielding represents a new frontier in defense against emerging threats.

Additionally, AI's ability to manage and automate cybersecurity tasks strengthens the role of Faraday Cages in protecting physical infrastructure. The use of AI to monitor network traffic, detect vulnerabilities, and respond to threats in real time ensures that Faraday Cages remain an integral part of a multi-layered security approach. This fusion of physical and digital security is essential in an era where both the virtual and physical worlds are susceptible to attack.

Personal Privacy and Faraday Cages

As national security measures become more advanced, the balance between protecting sensitive information and safeguarding personal privacy becomes a pressing ethical issue. While Faraday Cages are vital for securing government and military data, they also hold potential for ensuring personal privacy in an increasingly surveilled world.

The rise of global surveillance systems, data harvesting technologies, and mass surveillance by both state and non-state actors raises concerns about privacy and individual freedom. Faraday Cages, integrated with AI, offer a solution by enabling personal data protection against unauthorized monitoring. AI-driven Faraday Cages could be used to protect personal communication devices, such as smartphones, laptops, and wearables, from electromagnetic spying.

The application of Faraday Cages in personal privacy protection could also be used in public spaces—ensuring that data transmitted by IoT devices, personal assistants, and wearable tech is shielded from unauthorized surveillance or interception. With AI-enabled monitoring, these privacy-enhancing technologies would not only block external interference but also ensure that private data remains encrypted and secure.

Conclusion: National Security in the Age of AI and Faraday Cages

As the world continues to advance into a new era of technological complexity, the role of Faraday Cages in safeguarding national security will only grow more significant. The combination of Faraday Cages and AI offers unprecedented protection against electromagnetic threats, cyberattacks, and data breaches. By integrating advanced shielding technologies with AI's ability to predict, monitor, and respond to evolving threats, nations can build a more resilient defense infrastructure.

However, as with any technology, the ethical implications of these advancements must be considered. The intersection of national security, personal privacy, and AI-driven Faraday Cage technologies requires a balanced approach that prioritizes both security and individual rights. Moving forward, the symbiosis between Faraday Cages, AI, and national security will define the safety and privacy of future generations.

In the next chapter, we will explore the challenges and opportunities presented by personal privacy solutions using Faraday Cages, highlighting how individuals and organizations can use AI to automate their privacy protection and safeguard their digital lives.

Chapter 8: Personal Privacy and Faraday Cages

In an era where digital footprints are ubiquitous and surveillance is a constant concern, the need for personal privacy has never been greater. With the advancement of interconnected devices, smart technologies, and the growth of the Internet of Things (IoT), the line between public and private has become increasingly blurred. Faraday Cages, when integrated with Artificial Intelligence (AI), represent a powerful solution for individuals looking to protect their personal data and shield themselves from both cyber and physical threats. This chapter explores the intersection of Faraday Cages, AI, and personal privacy, focusing on how these technologies can safeguard individuals from unwanted surveillance, data breaches, and electromagnetic interference.

The Need for Personal Protection from EMF and Cyber Surveillance

As our lives become more digitized, the risks associated with electromagnetic fields (EMF) and cyber surveillance also grow. Mobile phones, laptops, wearables, and other connected devices emit electromagnetic radiation that can be intercepted, tracked, or even used for malicious purposes. These devices not only expose us to potential health risks from prolonged EMF exposure but also leave us vulnerable to digital espionage.

Personal privacy is under constant threat, with unauthorized entities gaining access to private data through both technological means and physical surveillance. For instance, malicious actors can use techniques such as electromagnetic eavesdropping or "side-channel" attacks to capture information from devices, even without direct access to the device itself. Additionally, cyberattacks can result in personal data theft, identity fraud, and privacy violations.

Faraday Cages, when applied to personal devices, offer an effective physical barrier against these threats. By blocking external electromagnetic fields and radiation, Faraday Cages ensure that signals from devices—such as cell phones, laptops, and other wireless gadgets—cannot be accessed or intercepted. However, the integration of Faraday Cages with AI takes this protective capability to the next level, offering dynamic and adaptive solutions for safeguarding personal privacy in real-time.

Using Faraday Cages for Data Privacy and Personal Security

At its core, a Faraday Cage acts as a protective shield, preventing electromagnetic waves from penetrating or escaping. When applied to personal devices, this shielding ensures that electromagnetic signals (such as those used for mobile communication, Wi-Fi, or Bluetooth) cannot be intercepted by unauthorized parties. For example, a smartphone placed inside a Faraday Cage will not emit a signal, rendering it invisible to external tracking devices.

The AI-enhanced Faraday Cage system goes beyond passive protection. AI can be used to monitor the electromagnetic environment around the shielded device, ensuring that no unauthorized attempts to access or interfere with the device go undetected. For instance, if a rogue surveillance device or hacking tool tries to scan the surrounding environment for signals, the AI system can detect the anomaly and trigger additional protective measures—like activating a more secure layer of shielding or issuing an alert to the user.

AI also allows for personalized security protocols, dynamically adjusting shielding strength based on the level of threat detected. For example, if you are in a high-risk location, such as a government building or conference where sensitive discussions are taking place, the AI can automatically strengthen the Faraday Cage's shielding capacity to offer maximum protection.

Moreover, AI-driven systems can assess and predict the potential risks posed by nearby electromagnetic radiation sources, such as public Wi-Fi networks or nearby 5G towers. Based on this information, the AI system can recommend or implement actions to reduce exposure or block certain signals entirely, enhancing your privacy further.

AI's Role in Automating Personal Privacy Solutions

One of the biggest challenges to maintaining privacy in today's hyper-connected world is the complexity of managing multiple devices and securing various channels of communication. As the number of personal smart devices increases, so does the challenge of ensuring that they remain protected against potential surveillance and data breaches.

AI plays a crucial role in automating personal privacy solutions, making it easier for individuals to secure their devices and data without needing deep technical expertise. For example, AI-powered Faraday Cage systems can autonomously detect when a device is at risk of being compromised by electromagnetic interference or unauthorized scanning. Based on real-time analysis, AI can initiate the appropriate response—whether that involves creating a temporary shield, alerting the user, or even disabling certain device features to prevent data leakage.

These systems can also manage and configure the settings of personal privacy devices, such as signal-blocking cases or RF shields, based on contextual factors like location, time, and user preferences. If an individual enters a location that is known to be a hotspot for surveillance—like an airport, public event, or even a crowded city street—the AI can trigger an automatic privacy mode that enhances protection for the duration of the visit.

Creating AI–Enhanced Personal Privacy Systems

AI can also be used to create more sophisticated personal privacy systems that go beyond simple shielding. These systems could involve the integration of multiple technologies such as biometrics, location tracking, and even machine learning to analyze user behavior and predict privacy risks.

For example, AI can be incorporated into smart home systems to ensure that electromagnetic fields do not interfere with the privacy of residents. The system could analyze the electromagnetic activity in the home and determine if there are any abnormal signals or potential surveillance attempts. If such an intrusion is detected, the AI could automatically activate Faraday shielding for the home network or alert the residents about the threat.

Additionally, AI can be employed to create privacy-enhancing protocols for wearable devices, such as fitness trackers or smartwatches. These devices are often connected to cloud services and can reveal a lot of personal information. With AI, these devices could be programmed to activate Faraday shielding when they detect that a user is entering a privacy-sensitive situation, such as a medical appointment, personal discussion, or secure environment.

In the future, AI may also be integrated with advanced encryption algorithms to secure the data transmitted by personal devices, ensuring that even if a device is compromised, the data remains unreadable without the proper keys or authentication.

Innovations in Consumer Electronics

The application of Faraday Cages for personal privacy is not limited to a few niche products. Increasingly, consumer electronics are being designed with built-in shielding solutions, driven by both growing privacy concerns and advancements in AI.

For example, smartphones, laptops, and wearable devices could soon come equipped with integrated Faraday Cages designed to block electromagnetic emissions when privacy is a priority. These devices could also be embedded with AI that adjusts the level of protection based on the user's behavior and location. Whether you are attending a sensitive meeting, traveling, or simply resting at home, AI could automatically assess your environment and adjust shielding levels to maintain optimal privacy.

As consumer awareness of electromagnetic exposure and surveillance risks grows, the demand for such privacy-enhancing technologies will likely increase. Companies that integrate AI and Faraday Cages into their consumer products will likely lead the way in creating the next generation of privacy-conscious electronics.

Building Smart Devices with Built-in Shielding

The future of personal privacy lies in the seamless integration of Faraday Cages into everyday devices. AI will play an essential role in making this shielding intelligent, adaptable, and user-friendly. Imagine a world where your smart home, smart phone, and even your car's communication system are all shielded from electromagnetic interference and surveillance by integrated, AI-powered Faraday Cages.

Such devices will be able to protect not only the device itself but also any data transmitted to or from it. For example, a smartphone might automatically activate a Faraday Shield when the user is at a public gathering, preventing location tracking or unauthorized data collection. Similarly, a car's navigation system could engage Faraday shielding when crossing through a potentially hostile electromagnetic environment, ensuring that vehicle communications remain secure.

Conclusion: Protecting Personal Privacy in the Age of Connectivity

As we move further into a connected world, where everything from our devices to our homes and vehicles is susceptible to digital threats, Faraday Cages—augmented by AI— are poised to become an essential tool in protecting personal privacy. Through the combination of electromagnetic shielding and intelligent automation, individuals can gain more control over their personal data, prevent unauthorized surveillance, and protect themselves from digital and physical threats.

However, as we embrace these technologies, we must also consider the ethical implications of their widespread use. How can we balance privacy and security with transparency and trust? What responsibilities do individuals and corporations have in ensuring that AI-powered privacy solutions are accessible and equitable? These questions will be critical as we continue to integrate Faraday Cages, AI, and privacy into the fabric of modern society.

In the next chapter, we will explore the innovations occurring within consumer electronics, detailing how AI-driven Faraday Cages are reshaping everyday devices to ensure that personal security and privacy are no longer afterthoughts but integrated features.

Chapter 9: Innovations in Consumer Electronics

In a world where digital connectivity defines much of our personal and professional lives, the need for privacy and security has never been more critical. We are constantly surrounded by smart devices—smartphones, laptops, wearables, home assistants, and even connected appliances—each one transmitting and receiving electromagnetic signals that can potentially be intercepted or exploited. This vulnerability is amplified by the exponential growth of the Internet of Things (IoT), which is creating an increasingly interconnected and open environment for data to flow.

At the same time, concerns over electromagnetic radiation (EMF) and its possible effects on human health are growing. While these concerns are not yet fully understood, there is no doubt that reducing exposure to EMF and securing the communication channels of our devices is essential. Faraday Cages, once thought of as a niche technology primarily used in laboratories and military applications, are now making their way into mainstream consumer electronics, providing a viable solution for both shielding and protecting privacy.

This chapter explores how Faraday Cages are being integrated into everyday consumer electronics, the role of AI in optimizing these innovations, and how these technologies are reshaping the way we think about security, privacy, and convenience in the digital age.

Faraday Cages in Everyday Devices

For most people, the concept of a Faraday Cage is still linked to large, cumbersome metallic boxes designed to shield sensitive equipment from electromagnetic interference. However, the potential of Faraday Cages is much broader, and with the rise of advanced materials and technologies, it's becoming increasingly feasible to integrate these protective shields into smaller, everyday devices.

Incorporating Faraday Cages into consumer electronics is a natural next step as we seek to balance the convenience of connected devices with the growing need for privacy and security. Smartphones, laptops, wearables, and even home appliances can now benefit from embedded Faraday Cages, which help to block electromagnetic radiation and prevent unauthorized access to data.

For example, one of the most common consumer applications of Faraday Cages today is in mobile phone cases. These specially designed cases feature a built-in Faraday shield that blocks electromagnetic signals, effectively rendering the phone "invisible" to external devices. This is especially useful in scenarios where users wish to maintain their privacy, such as preventing location tracking or blocking remote hacking attempts. When the phone is placed inside a Faraday case, it no longer emits a signal, and any incoming calls, messages, or data transmissions are intercepted by the cage rather than reaching the phone.

Similarly, smart home devices like thermostats, security cameras, and smart assistants can also be equipped with Faraday shields to protect sensitive data from unauthorized surveillance or hacking. In the future, it's possible that entire homes could be equipped with Faraday-enforced privacy zones, where all connected devices are shielded when not in use, allowing individuals to easily protect themselves from external monitoring.

Protecting Smartphones, Laptops, and Wearables

Smartphones are a prime target for digital surveillance. They constantly send and receive signals, making it easy for hackers, advertisers, or even malicious third parties to track users' movements, monitor communications, and intercept data. Protecting these devices from electromagnetic interference (EMI) and cyberattacks requires an integrated approach, and this is where Faraday Cages, combined with AI, play an essential role.

Mobile phone manufacturers are now exploring ways to integrate Faraday technology into the very design of their devices. For instance, some manufacturers have started incorporating metallic shielding materials directly into the body of smartphones, ensuring that even without an external case, the device is partially shielded from electromagnetic waves.

Laptops, with their constant connectivity and data processing, also stand to benefit significantly from integrated Faraday Cages. Laptops are often used to access sensitive information, and shielding these devices from unauthorized electromagnetic access can add an extra layer of security. As with smartphones, AI-powered systems can optimize the shielding process by dynamically activating or deactivating shielding based on the environment and risk level, ensuring that users are protected only when necessary, which can help preserve battery life and device functionality.

Wearable technology—smartwatches, fitness trackers, and even health monitoring devices—are increasingly becoming an integral part of daily life. However, many of these devices are vulnerable to privacy invasions, such as unauthorized data collection or remote hacking. By embedding Faraday shielding into wearables, manufacturers can protect sensitive health data from prying eyes. AI integration can further enhance these protections by allowing the device to autonomously adjust its shielding based on the level of risk it detects in the surrounding environment.

AI Solutions for Consumer Privacy Protection

The integration of AI into Faraday Cages in consumer electronics represents a massive leap forward in the ability to safeguard privacy and security. Unlike traditional shielding methods, which are passive and static, AI-enhanced Faraday Cages can continuously monitor the electromagnetic environment and adapt in real-time to potential threats.

For example, AI systems embedded within smartphones or wearables can continuously monitor surrounding EMF levels, analyzing factors like signal strength, frequency, and the presence of potential threats such as nearby surveillance equipment. When a threat is detected, AI can trigger the Faraday shield to activate, blocking any data transmission or reception. Once the threat has passed, the system can automatically deactivate the shielding, allowing the device to resume normal operations.

This dynamic form of protection is essential in today's world, where users are constantly on the move and need their devices to be both secure and functional. AI-powered Faraday shields can even prioritize threats, allocating more resources to higher-risk situations, such as when a user enters a high-security area or encounters a known source of surveillance.

Building Smart Devices with Built-in Shielding

In the future, we can expect to see even greater advancements in the design of smart devices that seamlessly incorporate Faraday shielding as part of their core functionality. This means that consumers will no longer need to rely on external cases or add-ons to protect their privacy. Devices themselves will come equipped with integrated shielding technology, offering users built-in security without the need for additional hardware.

For example, smart homes of the future may be designed to automatically shield all devices within a certain range, creating privacy zones that block EMF and prevent unauthorized data access. AI will manage these zones, dynamically adjusting shielding based on the specific devices present, the level of threat detected, and user preferences.

As the trend toward more integrated Faraday shielding continues, we can also expect to see the development of new materials that are both more effective and less intrusive. Advances in nanotechnology, for example, could lead to the creation of ultra-thin, flexible Faraday materials that can be incorporated into almost any device without affecting its form factor or performance.

The Role of AI in Device Optimization

AI plays a pivotal role not only in the activation and deactivation of Faraday shielding but also in the optimization of the shield itself. Through machine learning algorithms, AI can analyze vast amounts of data to predict the types of threats a device may face and adjust the shielding accordingly.

For example, by analyzing patterns in electromagnetic interference from nearby devices, AI can learn to anticipate potential risks before they occur. This predictive ability allows the system to react faster and more efficiently, reducing the risk of exposure. Additionally, AI can assess how much shielding is needed at any given time, balancing the device's performance with its security needs.

Machine learning models can also help improve the materials used in Faraday Cages, optimizing them for specific applications. For instance, in a high-frequency communication device, AI could suggest materials that offer the best protection against specific frequencies or types of electromagnetic radiation, improving the device's overall resilience.

Conclusion: Transforming Consumer Electronics with Faraday Cages and AI

As consumer electronics continue to become more integrated into our daily lives, the need for robust privacy and security solutions will only grow. Faraday Cages, once seen as specialized tools for scientific and military use, are now becoming integral components of everyday devices. The marriage of Faraday Cages with AI offers unprecedented levels of protection, not only from electromagnetic interference but also from digital threats such as hacking, surveillance, and data theft.

The future of consumer electronics is one where privacy is seamlessly built into the devices we use. With AI continuously working in the background to monitor, protect, and optimize, Faraday Cages will play an essential role in ensuring that our devices remain secure and our personal data stays private. As technology continues to evolve, so too will our understanding of how to balance the convenience of connectivity with the need for privacy—ushering in a new era of smarter, safer, and more secure consumer electronics.

In the next chapter, we will explore how AI-driven Faraday Cages can be used to enhance privacy and security across critical infrastructure, including data centers, hospitals, and communication hubs, where the protection of sensitive information is of utmost importance.

Chapter 10: Faraday Cages in Critical Infrastructure

In a rapidly evolving digital landscape, the protection of critical infrastructure has become a paramount concern. Hospitals, data centers, communication hubs, and other vital facilities are the backbone of modern society, ensuring the smooth operation of healthcare, commerce, governance, and communication. These infrastructures house sensitive data, facilitate mission-critical operations, and serve as gateways for information exchange. Given the increasing threats posed by cyberattacks, electromagnetic interference (EMI), and even natural disasters, safeguarding these environments has never been more crucial.

Faraday Cages, in conjunction with artificial intelligence (AI), provide a robust solution to protect these vital systems. Faraday shielding, by blocking unwanted electromagnetic signals and ensuring uninterrupted data integrity, is an essential tool in maintaining the safety, security, and functionality of critical infrastructure. AI's role in this context is to enhance the design, optimization, and operational monitoring of these protective systems, making them smarter, more responsive, and more adaptable to emerging threats.

In this chapter, we will explore the importance of Faraday Cages in protecting critical infrastructure, the role of AI in enhancing these protections at scale, and how these technologies come together to ensure resilience in an increasingly complex world.

Protecting Hospitals, Data Centers, and Communication Hubs

The healthcare, IT, and communications sectors are uniquely vulnerable to electromagnetic interference, which can disrupt services and lead to costly data breaches or operational failures. Hospitals, for example, rely on precision medical equipment, digital records, and real-time monitoring systems that must function without interference. A disruption in a medical device, whether caused by EMI or a cyberattack, can result in serious consequences, from incorrect diagnoses to delayed treatments or even life-threatening failures in critical systems.

Faraday Cages in hospitals can protect sensitive medical equipment, such as MRI machines, infusion pumps, and diagnostic tools, from external interference. AI-powered monitoring systems can optimize these Faraday shields, dynamically activating or adjusting shielding levels based on the surrounding electromagnetic environment. This ensures that interference from nearby devices, including mobile phones or wireless networks, does not compromise patient care or the accuracy of medical diagnostics.

Data centers, which house vast amounts of sensitive information, are also prime targets for electromagnetic threats. These facilities depend on continuous, uninterrupted service to store, process, and deliver data to businesses, governments, and individuals worldwide. A single electromagnetic disruption could cause catastrophic data loss, service downtime, or system failures, leading to a loss of consumer trust, financial damage, and legal implications.

Faraday Cages in data centers protect servers and communication networks from external electromagnetic interference. AI-driven systems can monitor and detect changes in the electromagnetic environment, triggering the activation of shields only when necessary, and optimizing power consumption and cooling efficiency. This AI-enabled dynamic shielding helps protect the integrity of the data without compromising operational efficiency.

Similarly, communication hubs that support essential services—like emergency response systems, financial transactions, or telecommunications—must be shielded from external threats. AI can continuously analyze the electromagnetic environment and adjust Faraday shielding to ensure that signals remain secure, while minimizing interference from natural or human-made sources.

The Role of AI in Enhancing Shielding at Scale

When it comes to critical infrastructure, scalability is essential. A single hospital or data center might have hundreds, if not thousands, of interconnected systems that need to be protected from EMI and cyber threats. Traditional approaches to shielding involve static Faraday Cages that are manually installed and maintained. However, these solutions are often impractical for large-scale environments where constant changes and updates are required.

This is where AI comes in. AI-driven systems can automate the detection of electromagnetic interference, predict patterns of potential disruption, and respond in real time to threats. Through machine learning algorithms, AI can also optimize the placement and design of Faraday Cages in large facilities, ensuring that all sensitive equipment is shielded effectively without the need for manual intervention.

AI's ability to process vast amounts of real-time data makes it possible to detect subtle patterns of interference that may go unnoticed by human operators. These systems can analyze data streams from thousands of sensors embedded throughout a facility and respond instantly to changes in the electromagnetic environment. This capability is crucial in preventing disruptions before they occur, and it ensures that protective measures are always active when needed.

In addition to real-time responses, AI can predict potential vulnerabilities based on historical data, usage patterns, and environmental factors. For instance, AI systems could forecast which areas of a data center or hospital are most likely to experience interference due to nearby electromagnetic sources, such as power lines or wireless communication towers. With this insight, AI can proactively adjust the Faraday Cages to shield these areas in advance, optimizing both security and performance.

Minimizing Vulnerabilities in Large-Scale Faraday Cage Systems

One of the challenges in implementing Faraday Cages on a large scale is ensuring that vulnerabilities are minimized and that the shielding remains effective over time. Large facilities are often complex, with numerous interconnected devices and networks, making it difficult to guarantee that every piece of equipment is adequately shielded.

AI plays a crucial role in identifying and addressing these vulnerabilities. Through continuous monitoring and data analysis, AI can identify areas where shielding is ineffective or where gaps may have developed. It can also predict the long-term effectiveness of shielding materials, helping facility managers optimize their investments in Faraday Cages.

For example, AI can be used to model how electromagnetic waves propagate through different materials and environments. By simulating various shielding scenarios, AI can predict how electromagnetic interference might penetrate existing Faraday Cages, allowing engineers to modify and improve the shielding in real time. This predictive capability is particularly important in ensuring that Faraday Cages continue to provide protection in the face of evolving threats, such as new types of electronic warfare or the increasing use of IoT devices that could generate unintended interference.

AI's Role in Disaster Recovery and Continuity Planning

The ultimate goal of Faraday Cages in critical infrastructure is to ensure resilience and continuity, especially in the face of natural disasters, solar storms, or other catastrophic events. AI can play a pivotal role in disaster recovery by enhancing the speed and efficiency of response systems.

For instance, in the event of a solar storm or electromagnetic pulse (EMP) event, AI-powered Faraday Cages can automatically isolate critical systems, preventing the overwhelming damage that could otherwise cripple essential services. Once the immediate threat has passed, AI can also help coordinate recovery efforts, reestablishing communication networks and restoring services to normal.

AI can analyze data from external sensors, weather reports, and other sources to forecast potential electromagnetic threats, allowing critical infrastructure managers to take preventive measures well in advance. This proactive approach can significantly reduce downtime and minimize the impact of disasters.

Moreover, in terms of continuity planning, AI can monitor the operational status of Faraday Cages in real time and alert facility managers to any breaches or weaknesses in shielding. AI-driven systems can also simulate different disaster scenarios to test the resilience of shielding and develop robust, responsive recovery plans.

The Global Impact of Faraday Cages and AI

As the world becomes more interconnected and dependent on digital technologies, the need for secure and resilient critical infrastructure is becoming a global priority. Faraday Cages, enhanced by AI, can protect not only individual institutions but entire nations by ensuring the stability of essential services during times of crisis.

Faraday Cages can protect not only local facilities but also international communication systems that depend on electromagnetic signals for secure information exchange. AI-enabled Faraday Cages can be deployed in international data centers, communication hubs, and power grids to provide real-time protection against global threats, such as electromagnetic warfare or large-scale solar events.

By creating a global network of AI-empowered Faraday Cages, nations can collaborate to protect critical infrastructure, safeguard sensitive data, and ensure continuity of services across borders. AI will play a key role in optimizing the deployment, operation, and maintenance of these systems, enabling a new era of global security that is resilient to both natural and man-made electromagnetic threats.

Conclusion: The Need for Smart, Scalable Protection

As we have seen, the role of Faraday Cages in protecting critical infrastructure is becoming increasingly important as digital connectivity expands. From hospitals to data centers and communication hubs, safeguarding these environments from electromagnetic threats is essential for maintaining the safety and security of our most important services.

AI is the key enabler that makes large-scale Faraday Cage implementation practical and effective. Through automation, predictive analysis, and real-time monitoring, AI is enhancing the design, optimization, and management of Faraday shielding systems, ensuring that critical infrastructure remains resilient in the face of evolving electromagnetic threats.

In the next chapter, we will explore the environmental impact of Faraday Cages, focusing on the sustainability of materials and practices used in their construction. AI's role in reducing the carbon footprint and creating green innovations in shielding technologies will also be examined.

Chapter 11: Faraday Cages in Space Exploration

Space exploration is one of the most thrilling and high-stakes arenas where Faraday Cages play a critical role in ensuring the safety and success of missions. As humans venture further into space, the challenges of protecting sensitive equipment and astronauts from the extreme environmental factors of outer space become increasingly complex. One of the primary threats is electromagnetic radiation, including solar flares and cosmic rays, which can severely damage electronic components, disrupt communications, and pose risks to human health. In this chapter, we will explore how Faraday Cages, enhanced by artificial intelligence (AI), are crucial in safeguarding space exploration missions—both on Earth and beyond.

Protecting Satellites and Space Stations from EMF and Solar Radiation

Satellites and space stations are critical to modern space exploration and communication. These objects are constantly exposed to a wide range of electromagnetic fields (EMF) and radiation, including intense solar radiation, cosmic rays, and charged particles from space weather phenomena like solar flares. These radiation sources can cause severe interference with sensitive electronic equipment, leading to system failures, data corruption, and even the destruction of hardware.

Faraday Cages provide an essential line of defense for these critical systems. By enclosing sensitive electronics within conductive shielding, Faraday Cages block out unwanted electromagnetic radiation, creating a controlled environment that preserves the integrity of equipment and data. However, the unique challenges of space environments necessitate more than just traditional Faraday shielding; the design and materials must be carefully chosen to withstand extreme conditions, such as fluctuating temperatures, vacuum conditions, and radiation from space.

AI plays a vital role in enhancing the design and functionality of these protective systems. Machine learning algorithms can be used to model how electromagnetic radiation interacts with various materials, helping engineers select optimal materials for the Faraday Cage that offer maximum protection without adding unnecessary weight. AI simulations can also predict how the shielding will perform in different space environments, adjusting for variables such as solar flare intensity, cosmic ray levels, and other radiation sources.

Moreover, AI-driven monitoring systems can continuously assess the performance of the Faraday Cages in space, ensuring they provide ongoing protection. These systems can detect any degradation of shielding over time or as a result of space weather events, triggering automatic adjustments or repairs to maintain optimal shielding effectiveness.

AI's Role in Designing and Simulating Space-Based Faraday Cages

Designing Faraday Cages for space missions requires specialized expertise and resources. Traditional testing methods, such as physical prototypes and manual trials, are often impractical in space, given the limitations of time and cost. However, AI offers a transformative approach by enabling detailed simulations that predict the performance of Faraday Cages under various conditions, without the need for physical testing.

AI algorithms can simulate how electromagnetic radiation interacts with the spacecraft's materials and the Faraday Cage structure itself. These simulations take into account the unique conditions of space—such as microgravity, temperature extremes, and radiation levels—allowing engineers to create highly effective shielding designs tailored to the mission's specific needs. Machine learning models can also be used to optimize the size, shape, and materials of the Faraday Cages, ensuring that they provide the necessary protection while minimizing weight, power consumption, and cost.

In addition to design optimization, AI can also enhance the manufacturing process. For example, AI-powered quality control systems can ensure that the materials used in Faraday Cages meet the stringent requirements for space missions. Machine learning algorithms can detect even the smallest defects in materials, allowing for the identification and correction of issues before they become problematic.

Shielding Astronauts from Radiation in Deep Space

Astronauts are exposed to levels of electromagnetic radiation in space far greater than those experienced on Earth. While the Earth's atmosphere and magnetic field provide natural protection from harmful solar radiation and cosmic rays, this protection is absent in space. Long-term exposure to these radiation sources can result in health risks for astronauts, including radiation sickness, increased cancer risk, and damage to the central nervous system.

Faraday Cages, integrated into spacecraft and spacesuits, are a key technology in protecting astronauts from these threats. In spacecraft, Faraday shielding can protect sensitive life-support systems, communication devices, and medical equipment from radiation interference. Additionally, small Faraday Cages or shielding layers can be incorporated into astronauts' suits, providing personal protection from space radiation during EVA (Extravehicular Activity) operations outside the spacecraft.

AI plays an instrumental role in the design, monitoring, and optimization of these shielding systems. For instance, AI-based simulations can model how radiation interacts with various materials used in astronaut suits and spacecraft walls. These simulations can identify the most effective combinations of materials and configurations that offer maximum protection against specific radiation types, such as solar particle events (SPEs) or galactic cosmic rays (GCRs).

Real-time AI-powered monitoring systems can also track radiation levels during missions, alerting astronauts and ground control if radiation levels exceed safe thresholds. In response, the AI system could automatically activate additional shielding, reconfigure existing barriers, or guide astronauts to more protected areas within the spacecraft. This level of adaptability is crucial for ensuring astronaut safety in the unpredictable and hazardous conditions of deep space.

The Future of AI-Powered Space Shielding Solutions

As we look to the future of space exploration, AI-powered Faraday Cages will be central to protecting both astronauts and the technologies that support their missions. With the ongoing push to explore Mars, establish lunar bases, and venture further into the cosmos, the need for effective and adaptable shielding will only increase.

AI has the potential to revolutionize space shielding by enabling autonomous systems that can not only design and optimize Faraday Cages but also adapt and evolve in response to new threats and environmental changes. For example, AI could drive the development of smart materials—self-healing or reactive substances that adjust their shielding properties based on real-time data from radiation sensors. Such advanced materials could respond dynamically to changes in radiation intensity, providing the highest level of protection at all times.

Moreover, AI's role in predictive analytics could be a game-changer. By analyzing data from previous missions, space weather forecasts, and even cosmic ray research, AI could predict when space radiation events are most likely to occur, allowing mission planners to take preventive measures or alter the spacecraft's trajectory to avoid dangerous radiation zones.

The integration of AI and Faraday Cages could also lead to the creation of autonomous shielding systems for future interplanetary spacecraft. These systems could monitor and adjust the spacecraft's protection in real-time, ensuring that it remains secure throughout long-duration missions. This would reduce the burden on human astronauts and ground-based engineers, allowing them to focus on other critical mission tasks.

Conclusion: Ensuring the Future of Space Exploration with AI and Faraday Cages

As humanity sets its sights on the future of space exploration, Faraday Cages will continue to serve as a foundational technology in protecting both equipment and personnel from the dangers of electromagnetic radiation and space weather. The convergence of Faraday Cages and AI holds immense potential for advancing space exploration, from shielding astronauts on long-duration missions to ensuring the continued functionality of satellites and space stations.

AI will play a crucial role in optimizing Faraday Cages for space, driving innovations in design, manufacturing, monitoring, and adaptation. With its ability to process vast amounts of data, simulate complex environments, and automate shielding adjustments, AI will empower space exploration missions to achieve greater levels of safety, resilience, and success.

As we move toward the next frontier of human exploration—whether on Mars, the Moon, or beyond—the synergy between AI and Faraday Cages will be one of the cornerstones of our ability to thrive in space. This partnership not only ensures the survival of our technological systems but also enhances the safety and well-being of the astronauts who carry the future of humanity into the cosmos.

Chapter 12: Faraday Cages in Healthcare

The healthcare sector has long been a critical area where technology intersects with human well-being. As healthcare systems become more reliant on digital devices, medical equipment, and real-time data collection, the need for robust protection against electromagnetic interference (EMI) and cybersecurity threats has grown substantially. Faraday Cages, combined with the power of artificial intelligence (AI), offer innovative solutions to safeguard both medical devices and patient data, ensuring that the evolving healthcare landscape remains safe, efficient, and secure. This chapter explores the pivotal role Faraday Cages play in healthcare and how AI is enhancing their effectiveness.

Shielding Medical Devices and Hospital Equipment

In modern healthcare, medical devices are essential for patient diagnosis, monitoring, and treatment. These devices—such as pacemakers, defibrillators, MRI machines, infusion pumps, and diagnostic tools—are highly sensitive to electromagnetic fields (EMF). Electromagnetic interference from external sources can lead to malfunctions, inaccurate readings, or even complete failure of critical systems. This can jeopardize patient safety and disrupt hospital operations.

Faraday Cages offer an effective solution to this problem by providing a shielded environment that blocks external EMF and radiation from interfering with medical equipment. Hospitals and clinics often utilize Faraday Cages or Faraday rooms to protect sensitive devices and ensure the uninterrupted function of essential medical technology. This becomes even more important as the adoption of wireless medical devices, such as remote patient monitoring systems, increases.

AI's role in enhancing Faraday Cages for healthcare applications is profound. For example, AI systems can continuously monitor the electromagnetic environment within a medical facility, ensuring that all devices are operating in a shielded space free from disruptive interference. These AI-powered systems can detect and locate any sources of electromagnetic radiation and automatically adjust or activate additional shielding to protect sensitive equipment. Furthermore, AI algorithms can analyze data from these systems to predict potential interference issues before they occur, preventing equipment failures before they disrupt patient care.

AI Solutions for Managing EMF in Healthcare Environments

Hospitals and healthcare environments are complex, with a wide range of electromagnetic sources, including diagnostic machines, therapeutic equipment, and wireless communication networks. Managing and mitigating the risks posed by electromagnetic fields is crucial for maintaining the safety and performance of healthcare systems.

AI-powered solutions can be used to map the electromagnetic environment of a healthcare facility and identify areas that require shielding or further protection. Machine learning algorithms can process data from EMF sensors distributed throughout the building, allowing them to identify patterns of electromagnetic radiation and predict areas of high interference. This predictive capability is especially useful in ensuring that the placement of Faraday Cages is optimized to shield equipment from potential sources of EMI.

Additionally, AI can help create dynamic shielding systems that respond to real-time changes in the electromagnetic environment. For example, if an MRI machine is in use, AI systems can automatically activate Faraday Cages or shielding materials around the room to block interference from other devices. These systems can also adjust shielding levels based on external factors, such as nearby electrical equipment or wireless communications, ensuring that the devices continue to operate at peak efficiency.

Protecting Patients from Electromagnetic Sensitivity

Some patients, especially those with specific medical conditions, may be particularly sensitive to electromagnetic fields. Electromagnetic hypersensitivity (EHS) is a condition in which individuals experience symptoms such as headaches, dizziness, and fatigue when exposed to EMF. While the scientific community continues to debate the causes and extent of EHS, it is clear that certain patients may require a more controlled environment to minimize their exposure to electromagnetic radiation.

Faraday Cages can play an essential role in protecting these vulnerable patients. By providing a physical barrier that blocks electromagnetic radiation, Faraday Cages help reduce exposure and improve patient comfort. In hospitals, this may involve isolating patients in shielded rooms or incorporating shielding into patient care areas such as private rooms and recovery wards.

AI systems can enhance these protections by monitoring patient environments and adjusting shielding levels based on real-time data. For instance, AI can adjust the shielding in a patient room if electromagnetic interference from nearby equipment is detected, ensuring that the patient's exposure is kept within safe limits. Additionally, AI can work in tandem with health monitoring devices to track and record symptoms related to EHS, providing healthcare professionals with valuable data to refine patient care.

Integrating Faraday Cages with AI in Healthcare Systems

The integration of Faraday Cages with AI technologies can revolutionize the way healthcare systems manage both EMF protection and cybersecurity. As the healthcare industry becomes increasingly interconnected, the potential for cybersecurity threats rises significantly. Faraday Cages not only protect medical devices from physical interference but also provide a secure environment for sensitive data and systems.

One of the most important applications of this integration is in the protection of healthcare data. Electronic Health Records (EHRs), medical images, and other sensitive patient information are vulnerable to hacking, data breaches, and electromagnetic interception. A Faraday Cage around a healthcare facility or data storage area can ensure that these data cannot be accessed via wireless signals or electromagnetic radiation, providing an extra layer of security.

AI can enhance this security by continuously analyzing the electromagnetic environment for potential vulnerabilities. Machine learning algorithms can identify unusual patterns in electromagnetic radiation, flagging potential security breaches or hacking attempts. For example, AI can detect the presence of unauthorized devices emitting EMF or wireless signals within a Faraday-shielded zone, alerting security teams to the presence of potential threats.

Moreover, AI can be used to automate compliance with health information security regulations, such as HIPAA (Health Insurance Portability and Accountability Act) in the U.S. By continuously monitoring the electromagnetic environment and assessing the effectiveness of Faraday Cages, AI can ensure that healthcare facilities adhere to strict data protection standards.

The Role of Faraday Cages in Healthcare Disaster Recovery and Continuity

In the event of a natural disaster, solar storm, or electromagnetic attack, hospitals and healthcare systems must maintain operations to protect patients and save lives. Faraday Cages can play a crucial role in ensuring continuity of care during such emergencies.

In disaster preparedness plans, Faraday Cages can be used to shield critical medical equipment and data systems from disruption caused by electromagnetic interference. AI can assist by managing the activation and monitoring of Faraday Cages during an emergency, ensuring that the necessary shielding is in place to protect devices from interference. Additionally, AI can help coordinate recovery efforts by analyzing real-time data and adjusting medical operations to respond to changing conditions.

For example, during a solar storm, which can induce powerful electromagnetic pulses (EMP), hospitals could activate their Faraday Cages and rely on AI systems to manage critical healthcare services. AI can predict which systems are most likely to be impacted by the storm and prioritize the shielding of sensitive equipment. In the event of a broader communication or power grid failure, AI-powered systems can help ensure that emergency operations continue by optimizing resource allocation and data flow within shielded environments.

Conclusion: Ensuring a Safe and Secure Future for Healthcare with Faraday Cages and AI

The convergence of Faraday Cages and AI technologies holds great promise for the future of healthcare. From safeguarding sensitive medical devices to enhancing cybersecurity and protecting patient privacy, these technologies will play an essential role in shaping a secure, reliable, and resilient healthcare system.

By integrating Faraday Cages into healthcare environments and leveraging AI for monitoring, optimization, and automation, we can ensure that medical facilities remain safe from electromagnetic interference, cyber threats, and environmental disruptions. As the healthcare industry continues to evolve and adopt new technologies, the combination of Faraday Cages and AI will provide a foundation for secure, high-quality care that protects both patients and healthcare providers.

The future of healthcare lies in embracing innovative solutions that safeguard technology, data, and human well-being. With Faraday Cages and AI working in synergy, the healthcare sector can navigate the complex challenges of the modern world, ensuring that both patients and medical professionals can operate in an environment free from electromagnetic threats and technological vulnerabilities.

Chapter 14: The Ethics of Faraday Cages and AI

As the technological landscape evolves, so too does the need to carefully consider the ethical implications of new innovations. Faraday Cages, when combined with artificial intelligence (AI), represent a transformative leap in shielding technology—offering unparalleled protection against electromagnetic interference (EMI) and cyber threats. However, like all powerful technologies, the integration of Faraday Cages with AI raises important ethical questions that must be addressed in order to ensure their responsible use. This chapter will explore the key ethical dilemmas surrounding the use of Faraday Cages and AI, focusing on privacy, surveillance, regulation, and the broader societal impacts of these technologies.

Balancing Privacy and Surveillance in a Hyper-Connected World

The increasing prevalence of AI and Faraday Cages is bringing about a fundamental shift in how we perceive privacy and surveillance. On one hand, Faraday Cages offer the promise of enhanced privacy by blocking unauthorized electromagnetic signals, thus securing data transmissions and protecting individuals from unwanted surveillance. On the other hand, AI-powered Faraday Cages can also be used to track and monitor the electromagnetic environment, providing an unprecedented level of insight into personal behaviors and activities.

The ethical challenge here lies in finding the right balance between protecting privacy and enabling necessary security measures. While Faraday Cages can block harmful or intrusive signals, AI technologies can also be used to track, analyze, and even predict human behavior based on electromagnetic footprints. For example, AI systems that monitor and control Faraday Cages in public spaces could potentially be used to gather sensitive data on individuals' movements, interactions, and preferences—without their knowledge or consent.

To navigate this ethical dilemma, it is essential to establish clear boundaries and guidelines regarding data collection, usage, and consent. Transparent regulations should govern the use of AI-powered Faraday Cages, ensuring that these technologies are only used for legitimate purposes and that individuals' privacy is respected. AI systems should be designed with built-in safeguards to protect against abuse and misuse, such as anonymization protocols and strict data access controls.

Ethical Dilemmas in Using AI for Faraday Cage Technologies

AI's role in Faraday Cage technology goes beyond monitoring and controlling shielding systems. AI also plays a pivotal role in the design and optimization of Faraday Cages themselves, through machine learning algorithms that predict interference patterns, select optimal materials, and simulate shielding effectiveness. While these capabilities significantly enhance the performance and efficiency of Faraday Cages, they also introduce ethical concerns about bias, fairness, and accountability.

For example, the AI algorithms used in Faraday Cage design might inadvertently favor certain materials or configurations that are not the most environmentally sustainable or that have hidden societal costs. Moreover, there is the risk that AI-driven Faraday Cage systems could be weaponized for purposes of mass surveillance, economic espionage, or even political control.

Ethical AI development in the context of Faraday Cages requires that we carefully consider the broader impact of these technologies. Developers should prioritize transparency, fairness, and accountability in the design of AI systems that influence Faraday Cage technologies. This includes ensuring that algorithms are free from bias, and that the decision-making processes behind AI-powered Faraday Cage solutions are explainable and traceable. Additionally, the environmental implications of Faraday Cage materials and their lifecycle impact must be factored into AI optimization models.

Regulating the Use of Faraday Cages for Personal and Corporate Interests

The use of Faraday Cages, particularly when coupled with AI technologies, raises important regulatory challenges. While Faraday Cages offer robust protection against cyber threats, their potential to block communication and control access to information also makes them a powerful tool for individuals and corporations seeking to protect sensitive data from external scrutiny. However, this same capability could be used to avoid legal or regulatory oversight, potentially allowing individuals or organizations to evade accountability for illicit activities.

Governments and regulatory bodies face the challenge of establishing frameworks that regulate the use of Faraday Cages without stifling innovation. The balance between protecting national security, corporate interests, and individual freedoms is a delicate one. Faraday Cages can be used to shield data centers, hospitals, or communication hubs from electromagnetic interference, but they could also be used to conceal illegal activities or subvert surveillance.

To address these challenges, regulatory frameworks must evolve to encompass both the technological capabilities of Faraday Cages and the ethical concerns associated with their use. For instance, it may be necessary to create specific regulations that govern the use of Faraday Cages in certain high-risk environments, such as financial institutions, government buildings, or critical infrastructure. These regulations should ensure that while individuals and corporations can benefit from the protection offered by Faraday Cages, they do not misuse this protection to undermine legal and ethical standards.

Creating Ethical Standards for AI and Shielding Technologies

As AI continues to play an increasingly central role in the design, optimization, and monitoring of Faraday Cages, the development of ethical standards becomes essential. These standards must address several key areas:

- **Accountability and Transparency**: AI systems in Faraday Cage technology must be accountable for their actions, with clear mechanisms in place for oversight and auditing. This includes providing transparency in AI decision-making processes and ensuring that their outcomes can be traced and understood by human operators.

- **Human Oversight**: Despite the potential of AI to optimize Faraday Cage technologies, human oversight remains crucial. AI should be used as a tool to enhance human decision-making, not replace it entirely. Ethical standards must emphasize that human operators are responsible for monitoring and making final decisions, particularly in high-stakes environments like hospitals, military installations, or critical infrastructure.

- **Security and Privacy**: Ethical AI systems must prioritize both security and privacy. Faraday Cages can protect individuals from electromagnetic surveillance, but AI systems monitoring these environments must ensure that the data they collect is used responsibly and does not infringe on individuals' privacy rights. This includes adhering to ethical guidelines on data storage, usage, and sharing, as well as ensuring that AI-driven privacy solutions are accessible and understandable to the general public.

- **Sustainability**: The environmental impact of Faraday Cages and AI systems cannot be overlooked. Ethical standards should encourage the use of sustainable materials in Faraday Cage construction and energy-efficient AI models. Given the potential global impact of widespread Faraday Cage deployment, the industry must prioritize sustainability alongside security and privacy considerations.

AI in the Future of Faraday Cage Innovation

Looking ahead, the future of Faraday Cage technologies and AI integration holds tremendous potential—if approached with ethical foresight. The next generation of Faraday Cages may involve autonomous shielding systems capable of dynamically adjusting to environmental changes, powered by AI that learns from its surroundings. This could have transformative implications for everything from personal privacy to national security.

However, as these technologies become more advanced, the ethical considerations will only become more complex. For example, the development of autonomous Faraday Cages raises questions about control and responsibility—if a Faraday Cage powered by AI prevents certain communications or activities, who is responsible for the decision? Is it the AI, the developer, or the end-user? These are questions that will need to be addressed as the field evolves.

Moreover, as Faraday Cages are integrated into emerging technologies, such as quantum computing, the potential for misuse could increase. Ethical guidelines will need to keep pace with technological advancements, ensuring that AI-driven Faraday Cage systems remain tools for good, promoting privacy, security, and sustainability without enabling exploitation or oppression.

Conclusion: Navigating Ethical Challenges with Responsibility and Innovation

The integration of Faraday Cages with AI technologies offers transformative potential across numerous industries. However, this potential comes with significant ethical challenges that must be addressed. By establishing clear, responsible ethical standards for the development and deployment of these technologies, we can ensure that they serve to protect individuals and society at large, rather than exacerbate inequalities or infringe on fundamental rights.

In the end, the ethical path forward lies in a careful balance of innovation, transparency, accountability, and respect for privacy. As AI and Faraday Cages continue to shape the future of technology, it is essential that we engage in thoughtful dialogue and make responsible decisions to navigate the complex ethical landscape that lies ahead. With the right balance, these technologies can be harnessed to create a safer, more secure, and more ethical world for all.

Chapter 15: Faraday Cages in Disaster Preparedness

Natural disasters and unforeseen events are part of the unpredictable reality we live in. As technology becomes more integrated into every facet of society, the vulnerability of critical infrastructure to both natural and man-made threats increases. One of the most significant threats in today's connected world is electromagnetic interference (EMI), which can be caused by solar storms, lightning, or even malicious electromagnetic attacks. In such a scenario, Faraday Cages—shielding technologies that protect sensitive systems from EMI—play a crucial role in ensuring that infrastructure, communications, and data remain secure and operational. This chapter explores how Faraday Cages, in conjunction with artificial intelligence (AI), can be used for disaster preparedness, offering solutions to protect communication systems and ensuring resilience and recovery in the face of crisis.

Shielding Against Natural Disasters and Solar Storms

Solar storms, also known as coronal mass ejections (CMEs), represent one of the most significant electromagnetic threats to modern infrastructure. These massive bursts of solar energy can disrupt satellite communications, GPS systems, power grids, and telecommunication networks. The electromagnetic pulses (EMPs) generated by such events can damage or destroy electrical components, leading to widespread disruptions that can last for days, weeks, or even months.

Faraday Cages are invaluable in mitigating the effects of such solar storms. By blocking out harmful electromagnetic radiation, these cages can protect vital equipment —such as communication systems, power generation facilities, and military infrastructure—from the damaging effects of solar flares. Faraday Cages have been used in space-based technology to shield satellites from radiation, and the same principles can be applied to terrestrial infrastructure, such as data centers, hospitals, and communication hubs.

AI can further enhance the protection offered by Faraday Cages. By using AI-driven predictive analytics, it is possible to monitor space weather patterns and anticipate solar storm events before they occur. Machine learning algorithms can analyze historical data to detect early warning signs of solar activity, allowing for timely responses to mitigate potential damage. Additionally, AI-powered systems can autonomously adjust shielding parameters based on real-time readings of electromagnetic activity, ensuring that Faraday Cages remain effective in dynamic conditions.

AI-Powered Disaster Response Systems

In the event of a disaster, response times are critical, and the ability to communicate and coordinate efforts is essential for saving lives and minimizing damage. One of the key challenges during large-scale emergencies is maintaining reliable communication networks. Often, traditional communication systems are overwhelmed or destroyed by the disaster, making it difficult for first responders and relief organizations to collaborate effectively.

Faraday Cages, coupled with AI, can play a pivotal role in disaster response by ensuring that communication systems remain protected from EMI, including that generated by solar storms, lightning strikes, or even malicious EMP attacks. AI-driven systems can automatically identify the most vulnerable communication channels and activate Faraday Cages to protect them. For example, emergency communication hubs, hospitals, and critical government facilities can be shielded from electromagnetic interference to ensure that essential services continue to operate without disruption.

Furthermore, AI can optimize the allocation of resources during a disaster. Machine learning algorithms can analyze data from multiple sources—such as satellite imagery, sensor networks, and social media feeds—to predict the most affected areas and provide real-time insights to decision-makers. By leveraging AI and Faraday Cages together, it is possible to create a resilient communication infrastructure that can withstand the challenges posed by natural disasters.

Using Faraday Cages for Emergency Communication Systems

In disaster scenarios, reliable and secure communication is the backbone of effective response efforts. From coordinating first responders to ensuring the safety of civilians, communication systems must be protected from interference. Faraday Cages can be deployed to shield communication systems, preventing them from being disrupted by electromagnetic interference (EMI) during emergencies. The use of AI allows for real-time monitoring and dynamic adjustments to shielding, ensuring that communication channels remain open even under extreme conditions.

AI-enhanced Faraday Cages could be used in key facilities, such as emergency operation centers (EOCs), hospitals, and military command centers, to protect their communication systems from disruption. These systems can automatically detect spikes in electromagnetic interference or a potential EMP event and immediately deploy shielding, ensuring the continuous operation of vital systems.

Moreover, in the event of a massive EMP attack or solar storm, Faraday Cages powered by AI could be activated across entire regions to protect infrastructure. AI algorithms would be able to assess which critical systems are most at risk and prioritize protection, thereby minimizing damage and enabling quicker recovery.

Building Faraday Cages for Resilience and Recovery

The ability to recover from a disaster is just as important as preventing it. Faraday Cages not only protect systems during a disaster but also help to ensure their rapid recovery afterward. Critical systems that are shielded from electromagnetic interference will continue to operate, enabling emergency responders to deploy and operate effectively, even when traditional infrastructure has been compromised.

AI can be used to assist in the recovery process by providing valuable insights into the performance of Faraday Cages in real-time. AI systems can track the status of critical infrastructure and alert operators if any system is experiencing disruptions or vulnerabilities. Additionally, AI can help coordinate repair efforts by identifying which systems are most critical for recovery and suggesting the most efficient path for restoration.

AI algorithms can also analyze the damage caused by a disaster and recommend improvements to Faraday Cages for future events. By integrating lessons learned from each disaster, AI can ensure that Faraday Cages are continuously optimized for resilience, making the infrastructure even more robust for future emergencies.

AI and Faraday Cages in Building Disaster-Resilient Infrastructure

Incorporating Faraday Cages into the design of disaster-resilient infrastructure is an important step in future-proofing cities, data centers, and communication networks. While traditional building practices focus on physical robustness, the integration of Faraday Cages adds an additional layer of protection against electromagnetic threats. AI can further enhance this design by optimizing materials, shielding configurations, and automated responses based on real-time environmental conditions.

AI tools can simulate various disaster scenarios, including solar storms, EMP attacks, and other electromagnetic disruptions, to predict the behavior of Faraday Cages in different contexts. These simulations can help engineers design more efficient and cost-effective shielding solutions, ensuring that critical infrastructure remains operational during and after a disaster. Furthermore, AI can automate the testing and validation of Faraday Cages, ensuring that they meet the necessary performance standards before deployment.

The Global Impact of Faraday Cages and AI in Disaster Preparedness

As climate change and global instability increase the frequency and severity of natural disasters, the need for robust disaster preparedness systems becomes even more urgent. The global implementation of AI-powered Faraday Cages in critical infrastructure could revolutionize the way we approach disaster preparedness. By protecting vital communication systems and other technologies from EMI, we can significantly improve our ability to respond to and recover from disasters.

On a global scale, AI and Faraday Cages can also be used to create more resilient international networks. As natural disasters increasingly transcend national borders, the need for cross-border communication and coordination grows. Faraday Cages, enhanced by AI, could be integrated into global communication systems to ensure that critical data and communications remain secure during emergencies. Additionally, AI-powered systems could facilitate the exchange of real-time disaster information across borders, ensuring that resources are allocated efficiently and effectively.

Conclusion: Securing a Resilient Future with Faraday Cages and AI

Faraday Cages, coupled with artificial intelligence, represent a powerful combination for ensuring disaster preparedness and resilience in an increasingly interconnected world. From protecting critical infrastructure against electromagnetic threats to maintaining secure communication channels during emergencies, the potential for these technologies is vast. As we face growing environmental challenges and an uncertain future, the integration of AI-driven Faraday Cages will be vital in protecting our societies, economies, and infrastructures from the impact of natural disasters and technological disruptions.

By incorporating Faraday Cages into disaster preparedness strategies and leveraging AI to enhance their functionality, we can build a more resilient future—one that is better equipped to withstand the growing array of global challenges. As we look to the future, the partnership between humans and AI, guided by principles of safety and sustainability, will be essential in safeguarding our world from the uncertainties of tomorrow.

Chapter 16: Legal and Regulatory Framework for Faraday Cages and AI

As Faraday Cages become more integrated into the fabric of modern technology, the legal and regulatory landscape surrounding their use, particularly in conjunction with artificial intelligence (AI), is evolving. The growing importance of AI and Faraday Cages in safeguarding critical infrastructure, ensuring personal privacy, and securing communication networks introduces a host of legal, ethical, and regulatory considerations. This chapter explores the complex legal and regulatory challenges that arise from the widespread deployment of Faraday Cages and AI-driven shielding technologies, offering insights into the frameworks that govern their use, compliance, and future development.

Understanding the Legal Implications of Shielding Technologies

The legal implications of using Faraday Cages in various sectors are multifaceted, ranging from privacy protection to national security concerns. Faraday Cages themselves are relatively simple technologies, but their applications—particularly when paired with AI—have far-reaching consequences. Whether used to secure military communications, protect personal data from surveillance, or shield IoT devices from cyberattacks, the deployment of Faraday Cages raises important questions about who controls access to protected spaces, how information is kept safe, and under what circumstances shielding technologies may be used.

From a privacy perspective, Faraday Cages are instrumental in preventing electromagnetic eavesdropping. This capability is critical for protecting confidential information, whether it's related to personal communications or sensitive corporate data. However, the widespread use of these technologies could lead to concerns about their misuse, such as creating "safe havens" for illicit activity or circumventing legal surveillance programs. Governments and regulatory bodies are tasked with establishing laws that balance the benefits of shielding technologies with the need for transparency, accountability, and law enforcement access.

From a national security standpoint, the use of Faraday Cages in military contexts raises additional legal challenges. Shielding military communications from electromagnetic interference is crucial, but these protections must be carefully regulated to avoid escalation of electromagnetic warfare, where rival nations might use similar technologies for hostile purposes. The legality of deploying Faraday Cages in military, government, and private-sector settings must therefore be scrutinized in light of international law, treaties, and defense policies.

AI-Driven Compliance and Risk Management

AI plays an increasingly significant role in compliance and risk management, particularly when it comes to the regulatory frameworks governing Faraday Cages. The ability of AI systems to monitor, detect, and respond to violations of legal requirements, such as unauthorized electromagnetic emissions or breaches of privacy, offers a powerful tool for ensuring that Faraday Cages are used responsibly and ethically.

One of the primary legal concerns with Faraday Cages is the unauthorized use of shielding to protect illegal activities, such as smuggling communications or evading lawful interception. AI-powered monitoring systems can assist in ensuring that Faraday Cages are not misused in this way by providing real-time analysis and reporting of electromagnetic activity within protected spaces. These systems can identify patterns of behavior that suggest illegal activity, such as attempts to shield devices from legal surveillance or interference.

Additionally, AI-driven compliance tools can be used to track and manage the deployment of Faraday Cages across various sectors, ensuring that they meet all relevant regulatory standards. For instance, regulatory bodies may require specific types of shielding materials, designs, or performance metrics for Faraday Cages used in certain industries (e.g., healthcare, defense, or telecommunications). AI tools can automate the process of verifying that Faraday Cages comply with these standards, reducing the risk of human error and increasing the efficiency of regulatory oversight.

Creating Regulations for Faraday Cage Usage and AI Integration

As the use of Faraday Cages expands, the need for clear and consistent regulations becomes more urgent. These regulations must cover a wide range of issues, from the design and construction of Faraday Cages to their use in cybersecurity, privacy protection, and national security applications. The integration of AI into the design, monitoring, and optimization of Faraday Cages adds a further layer of complexity, requiring regulators to adapt existing laws and create new frameworks that account for the technological advancements.

A key challenge is determining who is responsible for regulating the use of Faraday Cages and AI within different contexts. In some cases, national governments may take the lead in establishing regulatory standards for Faraday Cages in sensitive areas, such as defense, communications, and healthcare. International cooperation will also be necessary to ensure that these regulations are consistent across borders, especially given the global nature of digital communications and the interconnectedness of critical infrastructure.

Governments and regulatory bodies must collaborate with industry experts to ensure that regulations are both effective and feasible. For instance, regulations governing the use of Faraday Cages in consumer electronics (such as smartphones, laptops, and wearables) will need to strike a balance between security and usability. On one hand, Faraday Cages can help protect consumers from electromagnetic interference and eavesdropping; on the other hand, overly restrictive regulations could stifle innovation or create unnecessary barriers to entry for new technologies.

AI's role in this regulatory framework is to enable more dynamic and responsive governance. AI systems can help identify emerging risks and vulnerabilities in Faraday Cage technology and adjust regulatory guidelines accordingly. Furthermore, AI can assist in ensuring compliance through automated inspections, real-time monitoring of electromagnetic interference, and analysis of data streams to detect unauthorized use of Faraday Cages.

Global Standards for Electromagnetic Safety and AI in Technology

As Faraday Cages are used more widely across industries, global standards for electromagnetic safety will become increasingly important. These standards will govern not only the physical properties of Faraday Cages (such as shielding effectiveness and material specifications) but also the AI systems that enhance their functionality. International organizations, such as the International Electrotechnical Commission (IEC) and the Institute of Electrical and Electronics Engineers (IEEE), will play a key role in establishing these standards and ensuring that Faraday Cage technologies comply with best practices in electromagnetic protection.

At the same time, AI systems involved in Faraday Cage design and implementation will need to adhere to ethical guidelines and safety standards. For example, AI-powered design tools should not only optimize shielding performance but also ensure that the technology does not inadvertently create new risks or exacerbate existing problems. Ethical considerations surrounding AI's role in surveillance and privacy must also be addressed in the context of Faraday Cages. Regulations should clarify how AI should be used to monitor and manage Faraday Cages, ensuring that these technologies are not exploited for unlawful surveillance or control.

The Future of AI and Faraday Cages: A Unified Approach

The convergence of AI and Faraday Cages presents an exciting and transformative future for security, privacy, and electromagnetic protection. However, as this technology continues to evolve, it is critical to establish a legal and regulatory framework that facilitates innovation while safeguarding privacy and national security.

The future of AI and Faraday Cages lies in a unified approach that integrates technological advancements with comprehensive, forward-thinking regulations. Policymakers, industry leaders, and technical experts must work together to create standards that ensure Faraday Cages are used ethically, responsibly, and effectively. This approach will help ensure that these technologies fulfill their potential in securing communications, protecting personal data, and enhancing national security, while also preserving civil liberties and preventing abuse.

As AI continues to evolve, it will likely play an even larger role in the design, implementation, and monitoring of Faraday Cages, providing new ways to enhance their effectiveness and adaptability. AI-driven regulatory systems, alongside international cooperation, will pave the way for a secure, smart, and interconnected world in which Faraday Cages and AI technologies work in harmony to protect the privacy, safety, and integrity of individuals, organizations, and nations.

Conclusion: Legal Frameworks for a Secure Future

The development and deployment of Faraday Cages and AI-driven shielding technologies present significant opportunities for enhancing privacy, security, and resilience across multiple sectors. However, these technologies must be governed by robust legal and regulatory frameworks that address the complex ethical, security, and privacy concerns that arise from their use.

By creating clear regulations and standards for the use of Faraday Cages and AI, we can strike a balance between fostering innovation and protecting individual rights and societal values. As the global landscape continues to evolve, so too must the legal frameworks that govern these technologies. With thoughtful regulation and AI's continuous advancements, Faraday Cages can play a pivotal role in securing the future of a connected, technology-driven world while safeguarding our most fundamental rights.

Chapter 17: Faraday Cages in Disaster Preparedness

In an increasingly interconnected world, the role of Faraday Cages in disaster preparedness and recovery has gained unprecedented significance. Natural disasters, solar storms, and other unforeseen emergencies can disrupt communication networks, jeopardize critical infrastructure, and compromise public safety. The integration of Faraday Cages into disaster response systems, enhanced by artificial intelligence (AI), offers a powerful tool for mitigating the effects of such catastrophic events and ensuring the resilience of society's most vital systems.

Shielding Against Natural Disasters and Solar Storms

Natural disasters—ranging from hurricanes and earthquakes to floods and wildfires—have the potential to devastate entire regions. One of the less understood threats, however, is the impact of solar storms, or coronal mass ejections (CMEs), on electronic infrastructure. Solar storms can induce geomagnetic storms that damage satellites, disrupt GPS systems, and, more significantly, affect power grids and communication systems on Earth. The economic impact of such an event can be catastrophic, with recovery times measured in years, not months.

Faraday Cages are an essential component in protecting sensitive infrastructure from these electromagnetic disturbances. Their ability to shield electronics from electromagnetic interference (EMI) can prevent catastrophic failures of communication systems, power grids, and other critical systems during a solar storm. AI enhances this capability by enabling real-time monitoring of space weather and providing predictive analytics to determine when a solar storm might occur, allowing organizations to activate protective measures in advance.

For instance, AI systems can assess the level of solar activity and predict the potential severity of the impact on Earth's magnetic field. In conjunction with Faraday Cages, AI-driven systems can automatically switch on shielding protocols for vulnerable infrastructure, such as power stations, data centers, and communication hubs. The ability to predict and respond proactively to solar storms can significantly reduce the damage caused by these events, ensuring that vital services remain functional.

AI-Powered Disaster Response Systems

AI has become a cornerstone of modern disaster response, providing innovative ways to enhance preparedness, coordinate relief efforts, and protect critical infrastructure. When integrated with Faraday Cages, AI can improve the resilience of disaster response systems by enabling real-time data analysis and decision-making.

During a disaster, communications are often the first casualty, as power lines are downed, satellites are damaged, or radio signals are overwhelmed. Faraday Cages can protect communication networks from disruption, but the real power of these systems lies in their integration with AI. AI can process and analyze massive amounts of data from sensors embedded in Faraday Cages to assess the structural integrity of critical infrastructure, track the movement of disaster response teams, and ensure that emergency communications remain secure and uninterrupted.

AI can also play a vital role in managing the logistics of disaster response. By analyzing the real-time locations and needs of affected populations, AI can optimize the distribution of resources such as food, water, medical supplies, and personnel. AI-powered drones, guided by Faraday-Cage-protected communication systems, can be deployed to inaccessible areas to deliver essential aid, collect environmental data, or assist with search and rescue missions. The ability to keep these AI systems operational, even in the face of severe electromagnetic interference, is critical for saving lives and reducing recovery times.

Using Faraday Cages for Emergency Communication Systems

In the aftermath of a disaster, maintaining reliable communication is crucial for coordinating rescue operations, providing updates to the public, and restoring order. Faraday Cages, particularly those integrated with AI, provide an invaluable tool for ensuring that emergency communication systems remain functional, even in the most challenging environments.

Emergency communication networks, such as those used by first responders, law enforcement, and humanitarian organizations, are often built with redundancy and resilience in mind. However, when faced with significant electromagnetic interference, such as that caused by a solar storm or a man-made electromagnetic pulse (EMP), these systems can fail. Faraday Cages can protect communication hubs and equipment from these disruptions, ensuring that first responders can maintain contact with each other and with the command center.

AI can further enhance the functionality of these emergency systems by dynamically routing communication signals through the most stable channels and optimizing the allocation of bandwidth. AI-powered systems can also monitor the integrity of communication channels in real time, flagging potential vulnerabilities and rerouting traffic as needed to maintain continuous communication during a crisis.

Additionally, AI can automate the process of identifying and locating individuals in distress, facilitating faster and more accurate deployment of emergency responders. The use of AI in conjunction with Faraday Cages ensures that emergency communication systems are both secure and resilient, making them a cornerstone of any disaster preparedness strategy.

Building Faraday Cages for Resilience and Recovery

In addition to protecting communication systems, Faraday Cages can be integrated into the design of critical infrastructure to ensure its resilience during a disaster. Hospitals, data centers, power plants, and government facilities are all essential for recovery efforts. Without them, it would be impossible to coordinate relief efforts or provide services to affected populations.

Faraday Cages are particularly effective in shielding these facilities from external interference, allowing them to continue operating in the midst of a crisis. For example, AI-driven monitoring systems embedded within Faraday Cages can track the condition of electrical grids, water supplies, and medical equipment, providing real-time diagnostics to ensure that all systems are functioning optimally.

AI can also enable predictive maintenance, identifying potential vulnerabilities before they become critical issues. For instance, if a power plant is at risk of electromagnetic interference from an approaching solar storm, AI systems can automatically switch the plant into a protected mode, powered by Faraday Cages, to prevent equipment damage. In hospitals, Faraday-Cage-integrated AI systems can protect sensitive medical devices from EMI, ensuring that life-saving equipment continues to operate without interruption.

As part of the broader disaster recovery plan, AI-driven simulations can model potential disaster scenarios and assess the effectiveness of Faraday Cage installations in protecting infrastructure. This predictive capability allows decision-makers to invest in the most effective shielding solutions and ensure that resources are allocated efficiently.

The Role of AI in Building Disaster-Resilient Communities

Disaster resilience is not limited to protecting critical infrastructure; it extends to ensuring that entire communities can survive and thrive in the face of unexpected challenges. The integration of Faraday Cages with AI can enhance the resilience of communities by improving their ability to respond to emergencies, communicate effectively, and maintain essential services during and after a disaster.

Smart cities, powered by AI and enhanced by Faraday Cages, can be designed with built-in resilience to a wide range of disaster scenarios. AI can monitor environmental conditions, predict natural disasters, and provide early warnings to residents, allowing them to take proactive measures. When disasters strike, Faraday Cages in key infrastructure—such as hospitals, transportation networks, and emergency communication centers—ensure that these systems remain functional, providing a stable foundation for recovery.

Furthermore, Faraday Cages and AI can help manage resources more effectively in the aftermath of a disaster. AI-powered systems can assess the needs of affected populations, track the availability of resources, and coordinate the distribution of aid. This system not only ensures a faster recovery but also helps prevent resource shortages and distribution inefficiencies, which can exacerbate the crisis.

Conclusion: A New Era of Disaster Preparedness and Recovery

The integration of Faraday Cages with AI represents a groundbreaking shift in disaster preparedness and recovery. Faraday Cages provide critical protection for infrastructure, while AI enhances our ability to predict, respond to, and recover from disasters more effectively than ever before. Together, they form a powerful synergy that strengthens the resilience of society, ensuring that essential services continue to function even in the face of the most devastating events.

As the world faces an increasing array of natural and man-made threats, Faraday Cages and AI will be at the forefront of disaster preparedness, safeguarding the systems and networks that underpin our modern lives. With these technologies in place, we can build a safer, more resilient future—one in which communities, infrastructure, and critical services remain secure, even in the most challenging of circumstances.

Chapter 18: Legal and Regulatory Framework for Faraday Cages and AI

As the technological landscape evolves, so too must the frameworks that govern the use of emerging technologies such as Faraday Cages and artificial intelligence (AI). The interplay between shielding technologies and AI not only presents new opportunities for innovation and security but also raises significant legal, ethical, and regulatory concerns. These concerns include privacy, compliance, and international standards, all of which must be carefully considered as these technologies continue to reshape industries and societies.

In this chapter, we explore the complex legal implications of Faraday Cage technologies and AI integration, focusing on the need for clear guidelines, risk management, and the development of global standards for electromagnetic safety and privacy protection.

Understanding the Legal Implications of Shielding Technologies

The widespread adoption of Faraday Cages—especially as they integrate with AI-driven systems—presents a host of legal considerations that have yet to be fully addressed. These considerations are important not just for manufacturers and users of Faraday Cages but also for governments, regulatory bodies, and organizations that rely on electromagnetic shielding for security purposes.

Privacy Concerns

One of the most significant legal issues surrounding Faraday Cages is the protection of personal privacy. Faraday Cages, by design, block electromagnetic signals, including those used for wireless communication, location tracking, and data transmission. This means they can effectively shield individuals from unauthorized surveillance, which is increasingly common in a hyper-connected world. However, this ability to block signals can also create conflicts with existing laws around surveillance, particularly in contexts such as national security or law enforcement.

The use of Faraday Cages for personal data protection may conflict with regulations that require data sharing for public safety or criminal investigation. While these technologies offer individuals protection from unwarranted surveillance, they can also be used to obscure criminal activities. This creates a dilemma for lawmakers who must balance individual privacy rights with the need for national security and law enforcement activities.

AI complicates this further, as it can be used to automate and enhance surveillance measures, making it harder to track individuals who are using Faraday Cages to conceal their data. As AI increasingly plays a role in both surveillance and privacy protection, the challenge lies in creating a legal framework that respects both privacy and security.

Regulatory Compliance

For organizations that design, manufacture, and deploy Faraday Cages, complying with existing regulatory standards is essential to ensure that the technology functions as intended and meets the safety requirements of various industries. These regulations are particularly important in sectors such as telecommunications, healthcare, and military defense, where electromagnetic shielding is crucial to the security and reliability of operations.

Currently, the regulatory landscape for Faraday Cages remains fragmented. Different countries have different safety standards for electromagnetic radiation and interference, and Faraday Cages often must meet a range of specifications to be approved for use in sensitive environments. These requirements can vary depending on the material used, the design of the cage, and the specific purpose for which it is intended.

AI introduces additional complexity by making it possible to create custom, adaptive Faraday Cages. AI systems can optimize the design and material selection of Faraday Cages in real time, based on the environment in which they are deployed. This dynamic capability raises new questions about liability and certification. Who is responsible if an AI-driven Faraday Cage fails to protect against electromagnetic interference (EMI) or radiation? How can compliance be ensured for systems that are self-learning and capable of changing their operational characteristics over time?

These questions point to the need for updated regulations that take into account the evolving nature of AI and its role in Faraday Cage design and operation. Legal frameworks must be flexible enough to adapt to new technologies while still ensuring safety, security, and compliance with international standards.

AI-Driven Compliance and Risk Management

As Faraday Cages become more integrated with AI technologies, the need for automated compliance and risk management tools becomes more pressing. AI has the potential to revolutionize how organizations manage legal and regulatory risks associated with electromagnetic shielding. By using AI to monitor the deployment and performance of Faraday Cages in real time, organizations can ensure that they comply with local and international regulations and reduce the risk of costly violations or security breaches.

AI can help manage these risks in several ways. First, it can automate the process of monitoring and reporting compliance, ensuring that any changes in regulations are swiftly reflected in operational protocols. Second, AI can assess the potential risks associated with the deployment of Faraday Cages in various environments, evaluating factors such as electromagnetic interference, the potential for signal jamming, and the adequacy of shielding. Third, AI can identify vulnerabilities in the design of Faraday Cages, suggesting modifications to ensure they meet regulatory standards and provide optimal protection.

For example, AI-driven risk management systems can analyze the legal implications of deploying Faraday Cages in specific regions, taking into account local data protection laws, national security requirements, and environmental regulations. AI tools can also flag potential risks in real-time, alerting businesses to any changes in electromagnetic fields or environmental conditions that could compromise the effectiveness of shielding. These capabilities not only help organizations stay compliant but also reduce the likelihood of litigation, fines, or damage to reputation.

Creating Regulations for Faraday Cage Usage and AI Integration

Given the growing importance of both Faraday Cages and AI in safeguarding infrastructure, protecting privacy, and enhancing security, governments must develop comprehensive regulations that govern the use of these technologies. The development of such regulations should be guided by key principles such as transparency, accountability, and fairness.

Governments, working in tandem with technology developers, must establish clear guidelines for the responsible use of Faraday Cages and AI. These regulations should address:

1. **Transparency**: Clear standards for how Faraday Cages and AI systems are designed, tested, and implemented must be set. This includes guidelines for transparency in AI algorithms used to design and monitor Faraday Cages, ensuring that users can trust the system's decisions.

2. **Accountability**: Legal frameworks must clarify who is accountable for the performance of AI-driven Faraday Cages, particularly in sensitive environments such as hospitals, military bases, or critical infrastructure. Should a Faraday Cage fail to provide protection due to a design flaw in the AI system, who will bear responsibility?

3. **Privacy**: Given the growing concern about surveillance, regulations must ensure that Faraday Cages are used in ways that protect privacy without infringing on public safety. Clear rules should be established regarding when and how Faraday Cages can be used to block signals and data.

4. **International Coordination**: The global nature of technology means that regulatory frameworks for Faraday Cages and AI must be harmonized across borders. International bodies, such as the International Telecommunication Union (ITU), must develop global standards for electromagnetic shielding and AI applications. This would ensure that Faraday Cages are effective and legally compliant wherever they are deployed.

Global Standards for Electromagnetic Safety and AI in Technology

As Faraday Cages become an integral part of more industries, establishing global standards for electromagnetic safety is paramount. These standards must address the full spectrum of applications, from personal devices to large-scale infrastructure, ensuring that Faraday Cages offer effective protection without compromising safety or efficiency.

AI's role in shaping these standards cannot be overstated. AI-powered simulations and predictive models can play a crucial role in creating testing protocols for Faraday Cages, simulating various interference scenarios to determine the most effective shielding materials and designs. AI can also help refine these standards over time, based on real-world data and feedback, ensuring that they evolve to meet the growing challenges of electromagnetic interference.

Conclusion: Navigating the Future of Faraday Cages and AI

The legal and regulatory landscape surrounding Faraday Cages and AI integration is complex and still evolving. As these technologies continue to advance, it is essential for regulators, industry leaders, and technology developers to work together to create a balanced framework that promotes innovation while protecting privacy, security, and public safety.

Clear guidelines for the ethical use, deployment, and monitoring of Faraday Cages and AI will be essential for ensuring that these technologies contribute to the public good without overstepping legal or moral boundaries. By establishing a robust legal foundation, we can unlock the full potential of these technologies while safeguarding the interests of individuals, organizations, and society at large.

Chapter 19: The Future of AI and Faraday Cages: A Unified Approach

As the world moves toward an increasingly interconnected future, the symbiotic relationship between Faraday Cages and artificial intelligence (AI) will play a critical role in shaping the technologies that protect our privacy, security, and critical infrastructure. Faraday Cages are no longer seen merely as passive protective structures; with the infusion of AI, these technologies are evolving into dynamic, adaptive systems capable of responding to threats in real-time, learning from environmental conditions, and enhancing both human and machine capabilities.

This chapter explores how the fusion of Faraday Cages and AI will redefine security, privacy, and innovation in the coming decades, providing a glimpse into the future of shielding technologies and their impact on global systems.

Forecasting the Next Big Breakthroughs in Faraday Cage and AI Integration

The convergence of AI and Faraday Cage technologies marks the dawn of a new era in electromagnetic protection, one where static, rigid barriers give way to intelligent, responsive, and predictive systems. Several major breakthroughs are already on the horizon, which promise to revolutionize how these technologies are used.

1. AI-Powered Autonomous Faraday Cages

As AI becomes increasingly sophisticated, we can expect Faraday Cages to evolve from fixed, manually constructed units into autonomous systems. These AI-powered cages will have the ability to adjust their shielding properties in real-time, based on fluctuations in electromagnetic fields (EMF), interference, or environmental factors. Whether in a military communications hub, a data center, or a consumer device, AI will enable Faraday Cages to dynamically respond to external threats, optimizing performance without human intervention.

AI will utilize machine learning algorithms to predict potential interference events before they occur, adjusting the cage's shielding parameters in anticipation of those threats. For example, in satellite communications, AI could adjust the Faraday Cage around a satellite to prevent radiation interference from solar storms or space debris, based on real-time solar activity data.

2. Integration with Quantum Computing for Superior Shielding

Quantum computing, with its potential to exponentially increase computational power, is poised to impact nearly every field, including electromagnetic shielding. In the near future, AI and quantum computing could work hand-in-hand to create Faraday Cages that not only block unwanted radiation but also optimize electromagnetic environments for both devices and humans.

Quantum AI can model electromagnetic fields at the quantum level, predicting interference patterns with far greater precision than current technologies allow. With this enhanced computational capability, the materials and design of Faraday Cages will be optimized for performance on an unprecedented scale. These advancements will be essential for industries such as aerospace, defense, and healthcare, where electromagnetic shielding is critical to operations.

3. AI–Driven Real–Time Performance Monitoring and Adaptation

Future Faraday Cages will be equipped with AI-driven systems that continuously monitor and adapt to their environment. Using sensors and AI algorithms, these systems will track electromagnetic radiation levels, detect potential vulnerabilities, and proactively shield devices, infrastructure, and individuals. This real-time adaptation will enhance performance in both everyday settings and high-risk environments like hospitals or military installations.

These AI-powered systems will not only track electromagnetic interference (EMI) but also integrate with broader cybersecurity protocols. For instance, an AI-enhanced Faraday Cage in a data center could detect an attempt to bypass the electromagnetic shielding and immediately activate a response, securing sensitive data from external attacks. In autonomous vehicles, the AI could monitor the electromagnetic environment in real-time, ensuring that the vehicle's sensors and communications systems remain undisturbed by external interference.

4. Quantum-Resistant Encryption and Faraday Cages

In tandem with AI-driven Faraday Cages, the development of quantum-resistant encryption will provide an additional layer of security. As quantum computing makes traditional encryption methods vulnerable, integrating Faraday Cages with quantum-resistant encryption technologies will offer a unique solution to securing sensitive data against both digital and electromagnetic threats.

Faraday Cages, combined with AI, could not only block unwanted signals but also prevent unauthorized access to critical data by masking or scrambling communications. As quantum encryption becomes more mainstream, the ability of Faraday Cages to shield data and communication channels will be enhanced, making them an essential tool for safeguarding the next generation of information networks.

The Convergence of AI, Faraday Cages, and Sustainability

While the primary focus of Faraday Cages and AI has often been security and protection, there is a growing recognition of the need to integrate sustainability into these technologies. As the world becomes more environmentally conscious, it is crucial that the future of shielding technologies align with sustainable practices.

1. AI-Optimized Materials for Green Faraday Cages

In the quest for sustainability, AI will play a pivotal role in the development of new, environmentally friendly materials for Faraday Cages. AI-driven simulations can explore combinations of sustainable materials that offer the same level of electromagnetic shielding as conventional metals, such as aluminum and copper, but with less environmental impact.

For example, AI algorithms could identify plant-based composites or recycled materials that possess the necessary conductive properties, reducing the carbon footprint of manufacturing and operating Faraday Cages. Additionally, AI can assist in designing lightweight, flexible Faraday Cages that are easier to deploy in a variety of environments, from personal electronics to large-scale infrastructure projects.

2. Reducing Energy Consumption in Shielding Systems

As Faraday Cages evolve into smart, adaptive systems, AI will enable them to optimize their energy consumption, ensuring that the shielding process does not require excessive power. The AI-powered systems will adjust the energy use of Faraday Cages based on environmental conditions, such as the level of electromagnetic interference or the operational needs of a particular device. By doing so, they will ensure maximum protection while minimizing energy waste.

This energy-efficient approach will be particularly important in large-scale applications, such as in hospitals, data centers, and military installations, where energy consumption is a significant cost. Furthermore, as AI technologies continue to evolve, we can expect Faraday Cages to become integral components of green energy systems, working alongside renewable energy sources and smart grids to optimize their functionality.

3. Sustainable Design for Smart Cities

Smart cities, powered by AI and the Internet of Things (IoT), will benefit from integrated Faraday Cages that protect the vast array of connected devices from electromagnetic interference. These smart cities will need shielding solutions that are both efficient and sustainable, reducing the potential environmental impact while ensuring secure and uninterrupted communication channels.

AI-driven Faraday Cages will play a crucial role in creating these smart cities, ensuring that IoT devices, autonomous vehicles, and communication networks are protected from external interference. At the same time, AI will enable the sustainable design of these systems, ensuring that they are energy-efficient and use environmentally responsible materials.

How AI Will Shape the Future of Shielding and Privacy

The combination of AI and Faraday Cage technologies is not just about creating better shields against electromagnetic threats—it's about empowering individuals and organizations to take control of their privacy, security, and data. AI will enable a more personalized approach to privacy protection, with Faraday Cages that adapt to the needs of users, automatically shielding them from external interference and surveillance without compromising their access to necessary communication networks.

AI will also enhance transparency and accountability in the use of Faraday Cages. With AI algorithms continuously monitoring shielding effectiveness and data security, individuals and organizations will be able to verify that their systems are functioning as intended. Moreover, AI will provide insights into potential weaknesses in shielding systems, enabling proactive interventions before problems arise.

Conclusion: Embracing the Future of AI-Powered Security and Protection

As AI continues to shape the future of Faraday Cages, we are entering a new era of dynamic, intelligent shielding that will redefine how we protect our digital, physical, and personal spaces. The integration of these technologies will not only protect sensitive data and communication networks but also enhance personal privacy, promote sustainability, and strengthen global security.

The future of Faraday Cages is one of continuous adaptation, real-time monitoring, and seamless AI-driven optimization. As we move forward, it will be crucial to embrace these advancements in a way that balances innovation with ethical considerations, ensuring that these technologies are used for the greater good while safeguarding our fundamental rights.

By harnessing the full potential of Faraday Cages and AI, we can build a safer, smarter, and more secure world—one where both individuals and organizations are empowered to thrive in an increasingly complex, interconnected environment.

Chapter 20: Closing Thoughts on the Path Forward

The convergence of Faraday Cages and artificial intelligence (AI) marks a transformative chapter in the way we approach security, privacy, and technological innovation. This relationship is more than just a matter of shielding against electromagnetic fields (EMF); it represents a broader vision of protecting what is most vulnerable—whether that be our personal data, critical infrastructure, or even our human essence—from the accelerating threats of an interconnected world.

Throughout this book, we've explored the science behind Faraday Cages, their role in securing AI systems, and how the fusion of AI with shielding technologies offers unprecedented opportunities for growth, resilience, and protection. However, the journey has only just begun. As we look ahead, several key themes will shape the future of Faraday Cages and AI, each pointing to a unified approach where security, privacy, and technological progress are not merely aspirations but essential elements of our global society.

The Increasing Need for Integrated Protection

In a world increasingly reliant on interconnected devices and digital systems, the need for integrated protection has never been greater. Faraday Cages, long seen as passive enclosures, are now evolving into dynamic, AI-powered solutions capable of intelligently responding to a wide array of electromagnetic threats. From consumer electronics to sensitive military communications, Faraday Cages will serve as the first line of defense against cyberattacks, data breaches, and interference from both natural and artificial sources.

As AI continues to evolve, its ability to predict, respond, and adapt to electromagnetic threats will make it an indispensable tool for improving the effectiveness and efficiency of these shielding systems. This evolution will enhance the robustness of our digital infrastructure, enabling us to not only block interference but also optimize our interaction with the increasingly complex, data-driven world.

AI and Faraday Cages: A Blueprint for Sustainable Innovation

The integration of AI and Faraday Cages isn't just about security; it's also about sustainability. The growing demand for materials, energy efficiency, and environmentally conscious design will push the boundaries of what's possible in Faraday Cage construction. Through AI-driven simulations and predictive modeling, we will see a shift toward greener materials, reduced carbon footprints, and more energy-efficient designs. AI will allow for the development of adaptable, reusable shielding solutions that can be deployed at scale, ensuring that we address the challenges of both today and tomorrow.

From smart cities to autonomous vehicles, the future will demand that these technologies operate within a framework of sustainability. With the growing emphasis on the environmental impact of all industries, the combination of AI and Faraday Cages will help meet the need for security without compromising ecological responsibility. Whether through optimizing energy consumption or sourcing environmentally friendly materials, the synergy between AI and Faraday Cages will enable us to create a safer, more sustainable future.

The Role of AI in Personal Privacy and Empowerment

One of the most profound changes enabled by the marriage of AI and Faraday Cages will be the enhancement of personal privacy. In a world where our personal data is increasingly vulnerable to surveillance, hacking, and unauthorized access, AI-driven Faraday Cages will provide an innovative means of empowering individuals to take control of their digital lives.

AI-powered privacy solutions will automate the process of securing personal information, shielding our devices from unnecessary electromagnetic interference, and even managing our exposure to harmful electromagnetic radiation. Faraday Cages will move beyond passive barriers to become active agents in protecting our autonomy, providing peace of mind in a world where privacy is increasingly under siege. This shift will mark a turning point in the quest for personal security, enabling individuals to regain control over their digital footprint.

Ethical Considerations: Balancing Protection with Freedom

While the potential benefits of AI and Faraday Cages are vast, it is essential that we approach this technology with ethical considerations in mind. The very same shielding technologies that protect sensitive communications can also be used to curb freedom, stifle creativity, and limit access to critical information.

As we advance the development of AI-driven Faraday Cages, it is critical that we establish ethical frameworks that prevent the abuse of these technologies. Governments, corporations, and individuals alike must strike a balance between protection and freedom, ensuring that Faraday Cages are used to empower, not restrict. This will require ongoing collaboration among technologists, ethicists, and policymakers to create standards and regulations that safeguard privacy while ensuring that innovation remains unimpeded.

The Evolving Role of Humans in the Age of AI and Faraday Cages

Throughout this book, we have emphasized the evolving relationship between humans and AI. Faraday Cages, which have traditionally been seen as a protective mechanism, now serve as a symbol of how humans and AI can work together in a harmonious, symbiotic manner. AI is not here to replace human ingenuity but to augment and elevate it. In this new paradigm, AI is a tool that allows us to optimize and enhance our understanding of Faraday Cages and, by extension, the broader landscape of electromagnetic protection.

As AI continues to improve, humans will play an even more critical role in steering these technologies toward their ethical, responsible use. Faraday Cages may be automated, but it is the human element that will guide their application in ways that prioritize societal well-being, individual rights, and technological progress. We must recognize that, while AI offers great potential, it is ultimately humans who shape its direction and ensure that its impact is positive.

The Global Impact: A Collaborative Effort

The adoption of AI-driven Faraday Cages will have a far-reaching impact on global security and diplomacy. Faraday Cages are not just tools for individuals or corporations but essential elements of national and international security infrastructures. From shielding sensitive military communications to protecting critical global supply chains from electromagnetic disruptions, Faraday Cages will form the bedrock of digital diplomacy, trade, and defense.

The global nature of the challenges we face—whether cybersecurity threats, natural disasters, or geopolitical instability—requires a collaborative, multilateral approach. Countries and organizations must work together to establish standards, share knowledge, and pool resources in the development of AI-enhanced Faraday Cages. Only through collaboration can we ensure that these technologies are used to their fullest potential for the benefit of all.

Conclusion: The Path Forward

The future of Faraday Cages, powered by AI, is one of immense potential, marked by unprecedented advancements in security, privacy, and sustainability. As we look forward to this new era, it is crucial that we remain mindful of the ethical, social, and environmental implications of these technologies. The relationship between humans, AI, and Faraday Cages is not just one of protection; it is one of empowerment, responsibility, and growth.

In the years ahead, we will witness the transformation of Faraday Cages from static shields into dynamic, intelligent systems capable of anticipating, responding to, and mitigating the electromagnetic threats of a rapidly changing world. The union of Faraday Cages and AI will not only secure our digital futures but will also empower us to build a more resilient, connected, and sustainable society.

As we embark on this journey, let us embrace the potential of these technologies to create a safer, smarter future for all—one where the synergy of humans and AI ensures that we thrive, protected and empowered, in a world that is as complex and interconnected as ever before.

Chapter 21: The Future of AI and Faraday Cages: A Unified Approach

As we stand on the cusp of an extraordinary technological future, the intersection of Faraday Cages and artificial intelligence (AI) offers a unique opportunity to rethink how we protect, communicate, and interact with the world around us. This final chapter explores the potential of a unified approach to shielding technologies, where Faraday Cages and AI work in seamless harmony to protect our digital and physical environments from a growing range of threats.

The fusion of Faraday Cages and AI does more than improve existing security measures; it promises to radically transform the way we think about the role of protection in our increasingly connected and vulnerable world. By combining the historical principles of electromagnetic shielding with the cutting-edge capabilities of artificial intelligence, we can create an entirely new class of intelligent security systems that not only block electromagnetic interference but actively monitor, adapt, and respond to emerging threats.

Forecasting the Next Big Breakthroughs

The future of Faraday Cages lies not only in their passive role as protective barriers but also in their evolution into dynamic, AI-powered systems. Just as AI has revolutionized fields like healthcare, transportation, and communication, it is now poised to make significant strides in the way we design and utilize Faraday Cages.

We can anticipate the development of autonomous Faraday Cages—systems that not only detect and shield against electromagnetic interference but also make real-time decisions to adjust shielding strength and frequency based on changing conditions. This could be particularly beneficial in environments where electromagnetic threats are unpredictable, such as in high-security data centers, hospitals, or space stations. Faraday Cages will become "smart" enclosures, constantly learning from their environment and evolving to meet the needs of the moment.

The Convergence of AI, Faraday Cages, and Sustainability

Another critical area of future development is the convergence of AI and Faraday Cages with sustainability efforts. As we look to the future, there is growing recognition of the need to address the environmental challenges posed by advanced technologies. The construction of Faraday Cages, whether in personal devices, infrastructure, or space exploration, often requires specialized materials that may not be sustainable or environmentally friendly.

AI's role in material science and optimization offers a solution to this problem. By leveraging AI, we can accelerate the development of sustainable materials that are both effective at shielding electromagnetic interference and environmentally responsible. AI-driven simulations and material design tools will enable the creation of Faraday Cages that are lightweight, cost-effective, and built from recyclable or biodegradable materials, ensuring that their environmental impact is minimized.

Moreover, AI's ability to optimize energy consumption within Faraday Cages could contribute to reducing their carbon footprint. For example, AI systems could regulate the energy required to maintain a Faraday Cage, ensuring that the technology remains efficient without sacrificing protection. This focus on sustainability will make Faraday Cages a critical part of the broader push toward greener, more energy-conscious technologies.

AI-Powered Privacy and Security Solutions

As privacy becomes an increasingly important concern in a world dominated by surveillance and cyberattacks, the role of AI in enhancing the effectiveness of Faraday Cages will be paramount. AI can automate the process of personal privacy protection by identifying and blocking potential sources of electromagnetic interference that might compromise the confidentiality of communications or data.

For example, Faraday Cages in everyday consumer devices—smartphones, laptops, and wearables—could be augmented with AI-driven privacy features. AI would monitor the electromagnetic environment and automatically activate shielding whenever it detects an anomaly or potential threat. Additionally, AI could be used to create personalized privacy settings for individuals, ensuring that their devices are shielded at the right moments and in the right ways, based on their unique risk profile.

By incorporating AI into the privacy solutions of the future, we can ensure that individuals regain control over their personal information, reducing the risks associated with electromagnetic surveillance and cyber espionage.

AI in the Development of Autonomous Faraday Cages

As autonomous systems become more widespread, the role of Faraday Cages in protecting these devices from electromagnetic interference becomes even more critical. Whether in autonomous vehicles, drones, or smart cities, these systems will need to operate without the risk of disruption from EMF or cyberattacks.

The development of autonomous Faraday Cages will ensure that these vehicles, robots, and infrastructure remain safe from interference, while AI can monitor the performance of these shielding systems and adjust them in real-time. For example, autonomous vehicles will rely on AI-enhanced Faraday Cages to shield critical sensors, communication systems, and navigation systems from interference, ensuring the vehicle's safe operation.

Furthermore, these autonomous systems could be designed to integrate with broader AI-driven networks, where they will collaborate with other devices and infrastructure to share data about the electromagnetic environment. This could lead to the creation of "smart shielding networks," where Faraday Cages work together to protect entire cities, airports, or military installations from interference.

Quantum Computing and Faraday Cages

Quantum computing, a field poised to revolutionize technology, introduces both new opportunities and new challenges for electromagnetic protection. Quantum computers are extremely sensitive to external electromagnetic interference, which could disrupt their delicate operations. As quantum computing becomes more mainstream, the need for highly specialized Faraday Cages designed to shield quantum devices will grow.

AI will play a crucial role in advancing Faraday Cages designed for quantum environments. Through machine learning algorithms, AI can help simulate and design Faraday Cages that protect quantum computers from both external and internal sources of electromagnetic disturbance. Furthermore, AI-driven optimization algorithms will continuously improve the performance of these cages, adapting to the ever-evolving needs of quantum computing environments.

A Unified Approach: Integrating Faraday Cages with AI for Global Impact

The true potential of Faraday Cages and AI will emerge only when these technologies are integrated into a unified framework. Faraday Cages will no longer be seen as standalone entities but as part of a broader security ecosystem that incorporates AI's predictive capabilities, real-time monitoring, and intelligent decision-making.

This integrated approach will have a profound impact on global infrastructure. Governments, industries, and individuals will rely on AI-enhanced Faraday Cages to secure everything from military communications and critical data centers to personal devices and smart homes. The fusion of these technologies will create a more resilient, secure, and efficient world, where electromagnetic interference and cyber threats are mitigated before they can cause harm.

Conclusion: Embracing the Future with AI and Faraday Cages

The future of Faraday Cages and AI is not just about shielding us from electromagnetic interference—it is about creating a world in which technology, security, and privacy exist in harmony. As AI continues to evolve, it will transform Faraday Cages from simple protective barriers into intelligent, adaptive systems that actively respond to the ever-changing landscape of digital and physical threats.

Through a unified approach, we can harness the full potential of these technologies to build a safer, smarter, and more sustainable future. Whether in our homes, on the road, in the sky, or in space, AI-powered Faraday Cages will be essential in protecting our most valuable assets: our data, our privacy, and our future.

As we look forward to the next chapter in the evolution of Faraday Cages and AI, let us embrace the possibilities and challenges that lie ahead, working together to create a future where technology empowers, protects, and preserves our way of life.

Chapter 22: Legal and Regulatory Framework for Faraday Cages and AI

As the application of Faraday Cages and artificial intelligence (AI) continues to expand across various industries, it is crucial to establish clear legal and regulatory frameworks to ensure that these technologies are used responsibly, ethically, and securely. From the protection of personal privacy to the safeguarding of critical national infrastructure, the intersection of AI and Faraday Cages presents complex legal and regulatory challenges that require careful consideration. This chapter will explore the current landscape of legal frameworks governing electromagnetic protection, privacy, and AI technologies, and outline the steps needed to create a robust and globally recognized set of standards that can keep pace with technological advancements.

Understanding the Legal Implications of Shielding Technologies

Faraday Cages and AI-powered shielding technologies have significant implications for privacy, security, and intellectual property. As these technologies continue to be integrated into everyday products, their legal impact must be clearly understood and managed. The primary legal considerations for Faraday Cages and AI include:

- **Privacy and Data Protection:** One of the most pressing issues in today's digital age is the protection of personal information. Faraday Cages can play a critical role in ensuring that communications and data remain secure from electromagnetic eavesdropping, but their use may raise concerns about overreach, surveillance, and individual rights. The use of Faraday Cages to block EMF signals or prevent unauthorized access to data must comply with data protection regulations such as the **General Data Protection Regulation (GDPR)** in Europe or **California Consumer Privacy Act (CCPA)** in the United States. Regulations will need to ensure that the deployment of these technologies does not infringe upon privacy rights.

- **Intellectual Property:** With the rise of AI-driven design and optimization of Faraday Cages, intellectual property (IP) rights are a crucial consideration. Many AI algorithms used for optimizing Faraday Cages may be subject to patent protection, and companies involved in the development of these technologies must ensure they are properly protecting their innovations while also considering how to avoid infringement on others' IP.

- **Liability and Accountability:** As AI becomes more autonomous in its decision-making processes, questions about liability and accountability arise. If an AI-powered Faraday Cage fails to protect critical data or systems from electromagnetic interference, who is held responsible? Companies, governments, and developers must establish clear lines of accountability for any potential failures in these shielding technologies, especially when used in mission-critical applications.

- **National Security and Defense:** Faraday Cages have long been used for the protection of sensitive communications in military and government settings. However, with the introduction of AI into these systems, additional concerns about cybersecurity, espionage, and international relations emerge. The legal frameworks governing the use of Faraday Cages in defense and intelligence must adapt to account for AI's role in identifying and responding to external threats, which could range from hacking to electronic warfare.

AI-Driven Compliance and Risk Management

As regulatory requirements surrounding electromagnetic shielding and AI technologies evolve, AI can also play a key role in helping organizations comply with new standards and manage risks. By incorporating machine learning and AI-driven analytics into the compliance process, companies can ensure that their Faraday Cage designs and deployments are both legally sound and operationally effective.

- **Real-Time Compliance Monitoring:** AI systems can be used to continuously monitor and assess whether Faraday Cages and AI systems are in compliance with evolving legal requirements. These systems can analyze electromagnetic fields, data protection protocols, and communication security standards to ensure that all devices and infrastructure meet established legal benchmarks. For instance, AI could identify potential weaknesses in Faraday Cages that could compromise personal privacy or national security and suggest adjustments.

- **Predictive Risk Management:** AI can predict and identify emerging risks related to the use of Faraday Cages and shielding technologies. By analyzing large datasets of electromagnetic interference incidents, AI systems can forecast potential vulnerabilities in shielding designs and recommend proactive measures. In industries such as healthcare, military, and telecommunications, this predictive capability is essential for preventing costly or dangerous failures.

- **Automation of Regulatory Reporting:** For companies involved in the development and deployment of Faraday Cages, AI can automate much of the reporting and documentation process required by regulatory authorities. By tracking compliance metrics in real-time, AI systems can generate reports, flag potential issues, and ensure that all necessary certifications and audits are completed.

Creating Regulations for Faraday Cage Usage and AI Integration

The rapid integration of Faraday Cages with AI technologies calls for the development of clear, comprehensive regulations that can guide their use. These regulations should cover a broad range of considerations, including privacy, national security, intellectual property, and environmental impact. Key areas for regulatory attention include:

- **Standards for Faraday Cage Materials and Construction:** One of the first steps in developing regulations for Faraday Cages is creating universal standards for the materials and construction methods used in their design. These standards will ensure that Faraday Cages offer the level of protection necessary for their intended applications, whether in consumer electronics, data centers, or military facilities. AI can be a valuable tool in the development of these standards by simulating the effectiveness of various materials and designs under different conditions.

- **Safety and Environmental Guidelines:** As with all technological advancements, the environmental impact of Faraday Cages must be considered. The materials used in their construction—especially those in large-scale infrastructure—can have a significant carbon footprint. Regulations will need to mandate sustainable practices in the manufacturing and disposal of Faraday Cages, including the use of recyclable materials and the reduction of electronic waste. AI can help optimize the entire lifecycle of Faraday Cages, from material sourcing to end-of-life recycling.

- **Data Privacy Regulations for AI-Enhanced Shielding:** With AI-driven Faraday Cages becoming more prevalent, regulators must ensure that these systems do not inadvertently violate data privacy laws. AI-enhanced Faraday Cages must be subject to stringent regulations that prevent unauthorized access to personal data. This includes ensuring that AI algorithms used to manage shielding and security features do not themselves collect or misuse sensitive data.

- **Cross-Border Legal Considerations:** The use of Faraday Cages and AI for cybersecurity and privacy protection is a global issue. Different countries have different laws and standards regarding electromagnetic protection, data privacy, and AI. International cooperation will be essential in creating global standards that govern the use of these technologies, ensuring that they can be effectively deployed across borders without conflicting legal requirements.

Global Standards for Electromagnetic Safety and AI in Technology

To ensure the broad and safe adoption of AI-powered Faraday Cages, global standards for electromagnetic safety and AI integration must be established. These standards should be developed collaboratively by governments, industry leaders, and international organizations such as the **International Telecommunication Union (ITU)** and the **Institute of Electrical and Electronics Engineers (IEEE)**. These organizations can provide guidance on the best practices for electromagnetic protection, data security, and AI integration.

AI can play a central role in the development of these global standards by enabling the continuous evaluation of new technologies and their impact on public health, security, and the environment. As the use of Faraday Cages and AI becomes more widespread, ongoing research and collaboration will be necessary to ensure that these technologies meet the highest standards of safety, efficiency, and ethical responsibility.

Conclusion: Building a Safe, Secure, and Responsible Future

The future of Faraday Cages and AI integration will depend on creating a legal and regulatory framework that ensures these technologies are deployed responsibly. By focusing on privacy, security, sustainability, and international collaboration, we can build a world where Faraday Cages protect against electromagnetic interference while AI drives innovation in shielding, security, and compliance. As these technologies continue to evolve, the need for clear, adaptable legal frameworks will be more critical than ever in ensuring that Faraday Cages and AI work together to create a safer, more secure future for all.

Chapter 23: The Future of AI and Faraday Cages: A Unified Approach

The convergence of artificial intelligence (AI) and Faraday Cages marks a transformative milestone in the ongoing evolution of technology, security, and sustainability. As AI continues to advance, its integration with Faraday Cages opens new frontiers in shielding and protecting against electromagnetic interference (EMI), cybersecurity threats, and privacy breaches. The future of Faraday Cages, underpinned by the power of AI, holds incredible potential to shape a safer, smarter, and more resilient world. In this chapter, we will explore the unified approach between AI and Faraday Cages, how these technologies will evolve together, and their implications for the future.

The Convergence of AI and Faraday Cages

The synergy between AI and Faraday Cages is not merely additive; it is transformative. Faraday Cages, which have long been essential in protecting sensitive systems from electromagnetic interference, are now enhanced by the power of AI. This partnership offers the ability to create dynamic, responsive, and self-optimizing shielding solutions that can protect everything from personal devices to critical infrastructure.

AI enhances Faraday Cages in several ways:

- **Intelligent Shielding:** AI systems can monitor and adjust the effectiveness of a Faraday Cage in real-time, ensuring it is always optimized for the environment in which it is deployed. This could include adjusting for changes in electromagnetic interference (EMI) from nearby devices, or even responding to unexpected solar flares and other environmental factors.

- **Predictive Maintenance:** By analyzing historical and real-time data, AI can predict when a Faraday Cage might require maintenance or when a failure is imminent. This predictive capability can prevent costly downtime and ensure uninterrupted protection.

- **Optimization of Materials and Design:** AI can rapidly simulate different materials and Faraday Cage configurations, identifying the most effective designs for specific applications. Machine learning algorithms can take into account factors like material conductivity, frequency range, and shielding effectiveness, helping manufacturers create highly efficient and sustainable Faraday Cages.

This unified approach holds the promise of Faraday Cages that are not static, but instead evolve to meet emerging challenges—whether these are related to cybersecurity, environmental factors, or new forms of electromagnetic interference.

The Future of Faraday Cages in the Age of AI

In the near future, the use of Faraday Cages will go beyond traditional applications such as protecting military communications or shielding medical devices. With the rise of AI, Faraday Cages will become integral to securing a wide range of technologies, from smart cities to autonomous vehicles and IoT devices. Let's explore some of the key areas where the integration of AI and Faraday Cages will have profound impacts:

- **AI-Powered Smart Cities:** The cities of the future will rely heavily on IoT devices, autonomous systems, and real-time data flows. As the connectivity of these devices increases, so does the risk of electromagnetic interference, data breaches, and cyberattacks. AI-enhanced Faraday Cages will play a crucial role in creating safe, smart environments by shielding data from unauthorized access and ensuring the uninterrupted operation of critical infrastructure.

  For example, Faraday Cages could be embedded in the design of urban data centers, transportation hubs, and communication systems, providing a secure digital infrastructure. AI would ensure that these systems are adaptive, anticipating new threats and vulnerabilities in real-time.

- **Autonomous Vehicles:** As autonomous cars and drones become more widespread, they will rely on complex sensors, GPS systems, and communication networks to navigate and interact with their environment. These systems are highly susceptible to electromagnetic interference, which could compromise their performance. Faraday Cages will be integrated into vehicle design to shield these systems from external EMI, while AI will be responsible for monitoring the effectiveness of the shielding and ensuring the vehicle's safety and operational integrity.

- **AI-Driven Data Security and Privacy Protection:** With the increasing amount of personal data being generated by everything from smartphones to wearables, the need for robust data protection has never been more urgent. Faraday Cages, combined with AI-driven encryption and monitoring systems, will provide a powerful tool for safeguarding personal information. AI will not only optimize the shielding but also identify potential threats to data privacy and security, ensuring that data is always protected from electromagnetic eavesdropping and cyberattacks.

The Role of AI in Sustainable Faraday Cage Design

As the global focus shifts towards sustainability, AI will play a central role in developing environmentally friendly Faraday Cages. Traditional Faraday Cages often rely on materials that may not be recyclable or that have a high carbon footprint. The use of AI in material science and design will allow for the creation of sustainable Faraday Cages that minimize environmental impact.

- **Sustainable Materials:** AI will help identify and optimize the use of sustainable materials in Faraday Cage construction. By simulating the properties of various materials, AI can predict which are most effective at shielding electromagnetic radiation while also being environmentally friendly. These materials could include biodegradable or recyclable components that reduce the overall environmental footprint of the Faraday Cage.

- **Energy Efficiency:** AI can also play a role in reducing the energy consumption of Faraday Cages. For example, smart Faraday Cages could be designed to activate only when electromagnetic interference levels reach a certain threshold, reducing unnecessary energy usage. AI could also optimize the placement of shielding materials to minimize waste and ensure maximum effectiveness with minimal material use.

Quantum Computing and the Next Generation of Faraday Cages

As we look further into the future, quantum computing is poised to revolutionize the way we think about computing, encryption, and data security. Quantum computers operate at a level far beyond traditional computers, and they are particularly sensitive to electromagnetic radiation. This makes them vulnerable to both external interference and hacking attempts that could exploit their quantum state.

AI-driven Faraday Cages will become an essential component in the protection of quantum computers. These advanced Faraday Cages will be designed not only to shield electromagnetic radiation but also to interact with quantum systems in a way that preserves their delicate states. Quantum-resistant algorithms, developed and optimized by AI, will be incorporated into Faraday Cages to enhance their shielding capabilities against quantum-level attacks.

Moreover, the combination of AI and quantum computing could lead to new breakthroughs in Faraday Cage technology itself. AI-powered quantum simulations could help identify novel materials and designs that offer even more effective shielding against electromagnetic radiation, paving the way for the next generation of Faraday Cages.

Autonomous Faraday Cages: The Next Frontier in Protection

Looking ahead, we may see the emergence of **autonomous Faraday Cages**—shielding systems that are fully automated, self-optimizing, and capable of functioning independently. These autonomous systems would use AI to continuously monitor their environment, detect interference, and adjust their shielding mechanisms in real-time. This would be particularly valuable in dynamic and high-risk environments, such as military installations, secure data centers, and sensitive communication networks.

Autonomous Faraday Cages would be able to:

- **Self-Diagnose and Repair:** AI systems could autonomously detect when a Faraday Cage is malfunctioning or degraded and initiate repair processes, either through self-healing materials or through alerting human operators to perform maintenance.
- **Adaptive Shielding:** Depending on the level of interference detected, these Faraday Cages could automatically adjust their shielding power, optimizing energy usage while maintaining protection.

Building a Safer, Smarter Future

The integration of AI with Faraday Cage technology represents a unified approach to addressing some of the most pressing challenges of the 21st century, including cybersecurity, privacy, and environmental sustainability. As these technologies evolve and converge, they will provide unparalleled protection for individuals, organizations, and societies, ensuring that we can navigate an increasingly interconnected and vulnerable world with confidence.

The future of Faraday Cages and AI is not just about shielding against electromagnetic interference—it is about building smarter, safer systems that enable progress while safeguarding our fundamental rights. By embracing this unified approach, we are not only protecting our digital and physical environments but also laying the foundation for a more resilient and sustainable future.

In the end, the collaboration between AI and Faraday Cages represents the best of human ingenuity—intelligent systems working in harmony with our need for protection, privacy, and progress. The possibilities are limitless, and the journey is just beginning.

Chapter 24: The Global Impact of Faraday Cages and AI

The fusion of Faraday Cages and artificial intelligence (AI) is not just a technological breakthrough—it represents a profound shift in how we approach global security, privacy, and resilience. As the world becomes more interconnected, both digitally and physically, the need for effective shielding against electromagnetic interference (EMI), cyber threats, and privacy violations has never been more pressing. Faraday Cages, powered by AI, offer a transformative solution that is poised to affect not only individual privacy and national security but also the integrity of global trade, diplomacy, and communications.

In this chapter, we will delve into the global impact of AI-enhanced Faraday Cages, particularly their role in international communication systems, global security, and the protection of critical infrastructure. We will explore the ways in which these technologies are reshaping the world stage and enabling more secure and resilient networks for the future.

Faraday Cages in International Communication Systems

As digital communication networks evolve, so too do the risks associated with them. Governments, corporations, and individuals rely on increasingly complex and vast communication systems, which are vulnerable to a range of threats, including electromagnetic interference (EMI), hacking, and surveillance. Faraday Cages, designed to shield communication systems from external disruptions, play a crucial role in maintaining the security of international communication channels.

AI-powered Faraday Cages are revolutionizing the protection of global networks:

- **Global Encryption and Protection:** In diplomatic communications, military channels, and critical infrastructure, AI-enhanced Faraday Cages provide not just physical shielding but integrated encryption and cybersecurity protocols. These systems are capable of detecting electromagnetic threats in real-time, deploying dynamic shielding mechanisms, and encrypting sensitive data automatically to ensure secure transmissions.

- **Seamless Integration:** AI ensures that these Faraday Cages adapt seamlessly to the ever-changing electromagnetic landscape, adjusting shielding levels based on detected interference. In an era where cybersecurity threats are constant and evolving, AI's predictive capabilities will allow these systems to stay ahead of potential attacks and ensure safe, uninterrupted communication.

This dynamic synergy between Faraday Cages and AI provides an unprecedented level of protection for international communications, whether in high-stakes diplomatic negotiations, global financial transactions, or military operations.

AI-Enhanced Global Security through Shielding Technologies

The increasing vulnerability of global networks to cyberattacks and electromagnetic warfare necessitates robust security measures. The convergence of AI and Faraday Cages is reshaping global security strategies by providing advanced solutions to defend against the growing range of threats.

- **Electromagnetic Warfare Mitigation:** One of the most insidious forms of attack in modern warfare is electromagnetic warfare (EW), which seeks to disrupt, degrade, or manipulate communication and navigation systems through the use of high-powered electromagnetic pulses (EMPs). AI-driven Faraday Cages are capable of both shielding sensitive equipment from EMPs and actively detecting potential attacks in real-time. By utilizing AI to predict attack patterns and automatically adjust shielding, these systems significantly reduce vulnerabilities.

- **AI in Threat Detection and Response:** AI's role in global security also extends to its ability to analyze massive amounts of data and identify emerging threats in real-time. In conjunction with Faraday Cages, AI can monitor the electromagnetic spectrum, detect signs of intentional interference, and autonomously deploy countermeasures to protect critical systems from cyberattacks, hacking attempts, and data breaches.

- **Proactive Protection for Military and Government Assets:** In military and governmental contexts, AI-enhanced Faraday Cages are essential for protecting classified communications, military drones, satellite systems, and nuclear facilities from external threats. AI systems not only enhance the shielding capabilities but also ensure continuous monitoring, identifying subtle changes in the electromagnetic environment that could signal a cyberattack or covert surveillance attempt.

The result is a new level of proactive, AI-driven security that strengthens the defense capabilities of nations across the globe, ensuring the integrity of sensitive communications and infrastructure.

Mitigating Global Risks: Electromagnetic Warfare and AI Solutions

Global geopolitical instability and the rise of cyber warfare have brought electromagnetic threats to the forefront of security concerns. These risks range from targeted EMP attacks to more covert forms of interference that seek to disrupt and destabilize economies and governments.

AI-enhanced Faraday Cages are playing a crucial role in mitigating these risks by offering intelligent and adaptive protection mechanisms that are far more effective than traditional shielding methods. The combination of AI and Faraday Cages enables:

- **Preemptive Threat Neutralization:** With machine learning algorithms that continuously learn from global threats and patterns, AI systems can predict potential electromagnetic warfare scenarios and implement countermeasures before they escalate. Faraday Cages, driven by AI, can activate at the first sign of interference, ensuring immediate protection against electromagnetic attacks.

- **Dynamic Shielding for Large-Scale Systems:** For nations and large organizations, the scale of their critical infrastructure requires adaptable shielding solutions. AI-powered Faraday Cages can scale dynamically, adjusting to the size and complexity of different assets, whether they are communication satellites, data centers, or even entire cities. These solutions ensure that every aspect of the infrastructure remains protected, without any blind spots.

The Role of Faraday Cages in Protecting International Trade and Diplomacy

Global trade and diplomacy depend heavily on secure communication channels, and any compromise to the integrity of these channels can have far-reaching consequences. AI-enhanced Faraday Cages offer a robust solution for safeguarding sensitive negotiations, financial exchanges, and trade agreements.

- **Securing Digital Trade Routes:** As international trade increasingly relies on digital transactions and online platforms, AI-powered Faraday Cages ensure that data transmission remains secure from external interference. By integrating Faraday Cages into the core infrastructure of global trade networks, countries and corporations can protect financial data, sensitive contracts, and confidential communications from cyberattacks and espionage.

- **Diplomatic Encryption:** In diplomatic settings, where confidentiality is paramount, Faraday Cages combined with AI offer both physical shielding and encrypted communication. These systems can dynamically adjust to counteract any form of surveillance or hacking attempt, ensuring that sensitive diplomatic communications remain private and secure.

This combination of physical protection and AI-driven security is essential to maintaining the trust and integrity of international relations, especially in an era of heightened digital threats.

Integrating AI with Faraday Cages for IoT Security

The Internet of Things (IoT) is transforming industries, cities, and homes by connecting billions of devices globally. However, the more connected we become, the more vulnerable these devices are to electromagnetic interference, cyberattacks, and privacy breaches. Integrating AI with Faraday Cages provides a powerful solution for securing the IoT ecosystem.

- **Preventing Cyberattacks in IoT Environments:** IoT devices—whether in smart homes, healthcare systems, or industrial settings—are increasingly targeted by cybercriminals seeking to exploit vulnerabilities. AI-powered Faraday Cages can monitor and defend against attacks in real-time, ensuring that electromagnetic interference is mitigated and IoT communications remain secure.

- **Optimizing IoT Devices for Secure Communication:** By using AI to design Faraday Cages that are tailored to IoT devices, manufacturers can ensure that each device is shielded from the electromagnetic environment it operates within. AI can help optimize these shields based on device size, power needs, and communication frequencies, providing effective protection while minimizing energy consumption.

The role of AI and Faraday Cages in IoT security is pivotal in the creation of resilient smart environments, where devices remain interconnected but secure from external threats.

Conclusion: A New Era of Global Protection

The global impact of Faraday Cages, enhanced by artificial intelligence, marks a new era in the protection of sensitive systems, communications, and data. By integrating AI with Faraday Cages, we have the potential to build more resilient, secure, and adaptive networks that can withstand the growing threats of cyberattacks, electromagnetic interference, and privacy violations.

Whether in international diplomacy, global trade, or IoT security, AI and Faraday Cages provide an unparalleled level of protection that ensures the integrity of our digital and physical worlds. As these technologies continue to evolve, they will shape the future of global security, ensuring that we can navigate the challenges of a highly connected and vulnerable world with confidence and foresight. The future of Faraday Cages and AI is not just about shielding—it's about building a safer, smarter, and more secure global community.

Chapter 25: Legal and Regulatory Framework for Faraday Cages and AI

As the adoption of Faraday Cages integrated with artificial intelligence (AI) continues to grow across industries and sectors, the need for a robust legal and regulatory framework has become increasingly urgent. These technologies present profound implications not only in terms of security and privacy but also in how they impact national security, business practices, and personal freedoms. Legal considerations around the use, deployment, and management of Faraday Cages and AI must be carefully evaluated and balanced to ensure that their benefits are maximized while minimizing risks.

In this chapter, we will explore the legal implications of Faraday Cages and AI, the role of AI in compliance and risk management, the creation of regulations for these technologies, and the importance of establishing global standards for electromagnetic safety and AI integration.

Understanding the Legal Implications of Shielding Technologies

The integration of AI into Faraday Cages introduces new layers of complexity in terms of legal responsibilities, rights, and liabilities. As with any technology, the legal framework must address how these systems can be used ethically and within the boundaries of existing laws. Faraday Cages themselves are physical structures designed to protect against electromagnetic interference (EMI), but when AI is integrated into their design and function, new concerns emerge.

- **Intellectual Property (IP) Rights:** AI-driven Faraday Cages may involve the creation of new technologies, materials, and designs, all of which could be subject to intellectual property protections. Developers must navigate issues of patenting AI algorithms, shielding materials, and proprietary designs, ensuring that innovations are protected while respecting the intellectual property rights of others.

- **Liability for Failure:** One of the most pressing legal concerns with AI-enhanced Faraday Cages is the potential for system failure. While traditional Faraday Cages have been used for years to protect against electromagnetic interference, AI-enhanced systems introduce new risk factors. In the event of a failure—whether in military, healthcare, or communication applications—liability questions arise regarding who is responsible for the malfunction: the manufacturer of the Faraday Cage, the developers of the AI systems, or the organizations using the technology. Legal frameworks must address these concerns, establishing clear lines of accountability and mechanisms for redress.

- **Privacy and Data Protection:** The use of AI in Faraday Cages to monitor electromagnetic fields (EMFs) or protect sensitive communications also intersects with privacy laws. The collection, processing, and storage of electromagnetic data could potentially infringe on individual privacy rights, particularly when sensitive information is being shielded or monitored. Privacy laws such as the General Data Protection Regulation (GDPR) in the European Union must be considered when designing AI-powered shielding solutions. Ensuring that these technologies comply with data protection laws is essential in balancing technological advancements with privacy rights.

- **National Security and Export Control:** Faraday Cages, particularly in military and government applications, have national security implications. The use of AI in such systems adds an additional layer of complexity. Export controls on sensitive technologies, particularly those with AI capabilities, may restrict the dissemination of Faraday Cage designs to certain countries or regions. Legal frameworks must navigate these restrictions while facilitating innovation and ensuring security.

AI-Driven Compliance and Risk Management

As the deployment of AI-powered Faraday Cages scales, so too does the need for comprehensive compliance and risk management strategies. AI plays a crucial role in ensuring that these technologies are used responsibly and in compliance with relevant laws and regulations.

- **Automated Compliance Monitoring:** One of the most powerful aspects of AI is its ability to monitor and enforce compliance in real-time. In the case of Faraday Cages, AI can be used to ensure that the systems are operating within the established regulatory limits for electromagnetic interference, radiation shielding, and privacy protection. Automated systems can track whether Faraday Cages are meeting regulatory standards, generate reports for compliance audits, and flag potential violations before they occur.

- **Predictive Risk Assessment:** AI can also be leveraged to predict and manage risks associated with the operation of Faraday Cages. By analyzing large datasets, AI algorithms can identify patterns and trends that could indicate potential vulnerabilities in the system. This predictive capability allows for proactive risk management, enabling the timely deployment of countermeasures or system updates before a breach occurs.

- **Transparency and Accountability:** In order to comply with regulatory requirements, AI systems must also be transparent in their decision-making processes. The "black-box" nature of some AI algorithms presents challenges in understanding how decisions are made. However, for legal and ethical reasons, AI-driven Faraday Cages must be designed to ensure that their operations are auditable, traceable, and explainable. This transparency is critical for establishing trust and accountability in the use of these technologies.

Creating Regulations for Faraday Cage Usage and AI Integration

To ensure the responsible development and deployment of AI-enhanced Faraday Cages, governments and regulatory bodies must work together to create clear and comprehensive guidelines. These regulations should cover a wide range of issues, from design standards to operational protocols and safety measures.

- **Design and Safety Standards:** Regulatory bodies must set clear standards for the design and performance of Faraday Cages integrated with AI. These standards should specify the types of materials and configurations that are acceptable, as well as the minimum shielding effectiveness required for various applications. Additionally, safety protocols must be developed to govern the use of AI in Faraday Cage systems, particularly in sensitive sectors such as healthcare, military, and data centers.

- **Electromagnetic Exposure Limits:** One of the primary functions of Faraday Cages is to shield devices from harmful electromagnetic radiation. Regulatory authorities must define the acceptable exposure limits for electromagnetic fields in various environments, from urban settings to critical infrastructure. These standards will guide the development of AI-enhanced Faraday Cages to ensure that they meet public health and safety requirements.

- **Environmental Considerations:** As the environmental impact of technology becomes an increasing concern, regulations should also consider the ecological footprint of Faraday Cages and their AI systems. Sustainable materials, energy-efficient AI models, and eco-friendly disposal methods should be prioritized in regulations. This ensures that Faraday Cages do not only protect against electromagnetic interference but also contribute to broader environmental sustainability goals.

- **Cross-Border Regulations:** Given the global nature of technology and the interconnectedness of economies and industries, it is critical for regulatory bodies to collaborate across borders. International standards for electromagnetic safety, AI integration, and the use of Faraday Cages will facilitate consistency in regulations, allowing for a seamless flow of technology across markets while ensuring global safety and security.

Global Standards for Electromagnetic Safety and AI in Technology

The rapid advancement of AI-enhanced Faraday Cages calls for the creation of global standards to ensure uniformity in electromagnetic safety and the responsible integration of AI. These standards will help harmonize regulations across countries, facilitating international cooperation and trade, while protecting users from potential harm.

- **Electromagnetic Safety Standards:** The International Electrotechnical Commission (IEC) and the Institute of Electrical and Electronics Engineers (IEEE) are already working on setting standards for electromagnetic compatibility (EMC) and electromagnetic radiation. These standards will need to be updated to address the unique challenges posed by AI-driven Faraday Cages, ensuring that they provide effective shielding without violating global EMC limits.

- **AI Standards and Ethics:** As AI continues to evolve, global organizations such as the Organization for Economic Co-operation and Development (OECD) and the European Commission are working on frameworks for AI ethics and governance. These guidelines should be extended to cover the ethical use of AI in Faraday Cages, including transparency, accountability, and fairness in AI-driven decision-making processes.

- **Cybersecurity Standards:** The cybersecurity risks posed by AI-enhanced Faraday Cages, particularly in critical infrastructure, must also be addressed through global standards. These standards should ensure that AI systems are resilient to hacking attempts, that data privacy is maintained, and that there are robust mechanisms in place to respond to security breaches.

Conclusion: Shaping the Future of Faraday Cages and AI

As the use of AI-powered Faraday Cages becomes more widespread, the legal and regulatory landscape must evolve to keep pace. The development of clear legal frameworks, compliance systems, and global standards is essential to ensure that these technologies are used ethically, responsibly, and safely.

By creating regulations that balance innovation with safety, governments can foster an environment where Faraday Cages and AI can thrive—protecting sensitive data, enhancing national security, and preserving privacy in the digital age. The collaboration between legal experts, technologists, and policymakers will be crucial in shaping the future of AI-driven Faraday Cages, ensuring that they serve humanity's best interests while mitigating potential risks.